PRAYER VITALS

P9-AOO-474

Facts and Figures, Goals and Guidance

Tracy M. Sumner

BARBOUR
PUBLISHING

ISBN 978-1-61626-211-2

All scripture quotations are taken from the King James Version of the Bible.

Published by Barbour Publishing, Inc., P.O. Box 719, Uhrichsville, Ohio 44683 www.barbourbooks.com

Our mission is to publish and distribute inspirational products offering exceptional value and biblical encouragement to the masses.

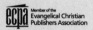

Member of the
Evangelical Christian
Publishers Association

Printed in the United States of America.

Contents

Introduction. .5

1. What's in *The Book*?: Some Biblical
   What's, How's, and Where's on Prayer . . .6

2. The Biblical Pillars of Prayer: The Five
   Different Ways God Wants You to Pray
   to Him. 32

3. From the Saints of Old: Some Biblical
   Prayers to Remember 48

4. Jesus: The Ultimate Man of Prayer:
   Christ's Teaching and Example
   in Prayer. 79

5. Some Great Sayings about Prayer:
   Quotations from Praying Men and
   Women 91

6. Some Prayers to Remember: Samples
   of Famous Prayers by Famous People. . . 119

7. Not Your "Everyday" Prayers: Prayers
   for Holidays/Special Occasions. 144

INTRODUCTION

Someone once said that praying is as natural to a human as breathing. And yet so few of us really know how to do it—at least in the way that God says to do it. In fact, the people who were the closest to Jesus—His twelve disciples—didn't have a clue how they should pray. That's why they asked Him one day, "Lord, teach us to pray!"

That's what this book is all about.

This book is a basically a collection of lists—some of them straight out of the Bible and some of them from other sources. Each of these lists has to do with prayer, either how to pray or how others have prayed in the past.

But this book isn't meant to be just a fun collection of information—even though we hope you enjoy reading it. It's meant to challenge you and to get you thinking about what it really means to pray. There isn't a lot of commentary on the scriptures, facts, or quotations we've included—we'll leave the interpretations and applications up to you.

1
What's in The *Book*?
Some Biblical What's, How's, and Where's on Prayer

Since the real message behind the stories, promises, and commands in the Bible is relating to God in a personal way, it only makes sense that His written Word would have a lot to say about prayer.

That it most certainly does!

This chapter is a collection of biblical advice, commands, promises, and wisdom on the subject of prayer. And while we couldn't get everything the Bible has to say about prayer to fit in this chapter, what you're about to read will give you some pretty solid guidelines for your life of prayer.

Some Biblical Prayer Trivia

- **The Bible's first mention of prayer:** "And to Seth, to him also there was born a son; and he called his name Enos: then began men to call upon the name of the LORD" (Genesis 4:26).
- **The Bible's first use of the word pray (in reference to speaking to God):** "My LORD, if now I have found favour

in thy sight, pass not away, I pray thee, from thy servant" (Genesis 18:3).

- **The Bible's first use of the word prayer:** "For thou, O LORD of hosts, God of Israel, hast revealed to thy servant, saying, I will build thee an house: therefore hath thy servant found in his heart to pray this prayer unto thee" (2 Samuel 7:27).
- **The Bible's last use of the word prayer:** "And the smoke of the incense, which came with the prayers of the saints, ascended up before God out of the angel's hand" (Revelation 8:4).
- **Number of verses that include the word prayer: 128**
- **Number of prayers in the Bible: approximately 650**
- **Number of answered prayers in the Bible: approximately 450**

PHYSICAL POSTURES FOR PRAYER IN THE BIBLE

- **Bowing heads:** "And the people believed: and when they heard that the LORD had visited the children of Israel, and that he had looked upon their affliction, then they bowed their heads and worshipped" (Exodus 4:31).
- **Standing:** "And Solomon stood before

the altar of the LORD in the presence of all the congregation of Israel, and spread forth his hands toward heaven" (1 Kings 8:22).

- **Kneeling:** "And it was so, that when Solomon had made an end of praying all this prayer and supplication unto the LORD, he arose from before the altar of the LORD, from kneeling on his knees with his hands spread up to heaven" (1 Kings 8:54).

- **On their faces before God:** "And Jehoshaphat bowed his head with his face to the ground: and all Judah and the inhabitants of Jerusalem fell before the LORD, worshipping the LORD" (2 Chronicles 20:18; see also Matthew 26:39).

PRAYER: ALSO KNOWN (IN THE BIBLE) AS. . .

1. **Bowing the knees:** "For this cause I bow my knees unto the Father of our Lord Jesus Christ" (Ephesians 3:14).
2. **Looking up:** "My voice shalt thou hear in the morning, O LORD; in the morning will I direct my prayer unto thee, and will look up" (Psalm 5:3).
3. **Lifting up the soul:** "Unto thee, O LORD, do I lift up my soul" (Psalm 25:1).

4. **Lifting up the heart:** "Let us lift up our heart with our hands unto God in the heavens" (Lamentations 3:41).

5. **Pouring out the heart:** "Trust in him at all times; ye people, pour out your heart before him: God is a refuge for us" (Psalm 62:8).

6. **Pouring out the soul:** "And Hannah answered and said, No, my lord, I am a woman of a sorrowful spirit: I have drunk neither wine nor strong drink, but have poured out my soul before the LORD" (1 Samuel 1:15).

7. **Calling upon the name of the Lord:** "And he removed from thence unto a mountain on the east of Bethel, and pitched his tent, having Bethel on the west, and Hai on the east: and there he builded an altar unto the LORD, and called upon the name of the LORD" (Genesis 12:8; see also Psalm 116:4; Acts 22:16).

8. **Crying unto God:** "Hear, O LORD, when I cry with my voice: have mercy also upon me, and answer me" (Psalm 27:7; see also Psalm 34:6).

9. **Drawing near to God:** "But it is good for me to draw near to God: I have put my trust in the Lord GOD, that I may

declare all thy works" (Psalm 73:28; see also Hebrews 10:22).

10. **Crying to heaven:** "And for this cause Hezekiah the king, and the prophet Isaiah the son of Amoz, prayed and cried to heaven" (2 Chronicles 32:20).

11. **Beseeching (pleading with) the Lord:** "And Moses besought the LORD his God, and said, LORD, why doth thy wrath wax hot against thy people, which thou hast brought forth out of the land of Egypt with great power, and with a mighty hand?" (Exodus 32:11).

12. **Seeking unto God:** "If thou wouldest seek unto God betimes, and make thy supplication to the Almighty" (Job 8:5).

13. **Seeking the face of the Lord:** "When thou saidst, Seek ye my face; my heart said unto thee, Thy face, LORD, will I seek" (Psalm 27:8).

14. **Making supplication:** "If thou wouldest seek unto God betimes, and make thy supplication to the Almighty" (Job 8:5; see also Jeremiah 36:7).

25 BIBLICAL PRAYER HOW-TO'S: WE SHOULD PRAY. . .

1. **In the Holy Spirit:** "Praying always with all prayer and supplication in the

Spirit, and watching thereunto with all perseverance and supplication for all saints" (Ephesians 6:18; see also Jude 1:20).

2. **In faith:** "And all things, whatsoever ye shall ask in prayer, believing, ye shall receive" (Matthew 21:22; see also James 1:6).

3. **With full assurance:** "Let us draw near with a true heart in full assurance of faith, having our hearts sprinkled from an evil conscience, and our bodies washed with pure water" (Hebrews 10:22).

4. **With a heart of forgiveness for others who have hurt us:** "And forgive us our debts, as we forgive our debtors" (Matthew 6:12).

5. **With all the heart:** "And ye shall seek me, and find me, when ye shall search for me with all your heart" (Jeremiah 29:13; see also Lamentations 3:41; Psalm 119:58).

6. **With a prepared heart:** "If thou prepare thine heart, and stretch out thine hands toward him. . ." (Job 11:13).

7. **With a true heart:** "Let us draw near with a true heart in full assurance of faith, having our hearts sprinkled from an evil

conscience, and our bodies washed with pure water" (Hebrews 10:22).

8. **With a poured out soul:** "When I remember these things, I pour out my soul in me: for I had gone with the multitude, I went with them to the house of God, with the voice of joy and praise, with a multitude that kept holyday" (Psalm 42:4).

9. **In the spirit and in truth;** "Ye worship ye know not what: we know what we worship: for salvation is of the Jews. But the hour cometh, and now is, when the true worshippers shall worship the Father in spirit and in truth: for the Father seeketh such to worship him. God is a Spirit: and they that worship him must worship him in spirit and in truth" (John 4:22–24; see also 1 Corinthians 14:15).

10. **With full confidence in God:** "When I cry unto thee, then shall mine enemies turn back: this I know; for God is for me" (Psalm 56:9; see also Psalm 86:7).

11. **With full confidence we are heard:** "And this is the confidence that we have in him, that, if we ask any thing according to his will, he heareth us" (1 John 5:14).

12. **With an attitude of submission to God:** "Father, if thou be willing, remove this cup from me: nevertheless not my will, but thine, be done" (Luke 22:42).

13. **Without use of deceitful lips:** "Hear the right, O Lord, attend unto my cry, give ear unto my prayer, that goeth not out of feigned lips" (Psalm 17:1).

14. **Thoughtfully:** "Be not rash with thy mouth, and let not thine heart be hasty to utter any thing before God: for God is in heaven, and thou upon earth: therefore let thy words be few" (Ecclesiastes 5:2).

15. **With holiness:** "I will therefore that men pray every where, lifting up holy hands, without wrath and doubting" (1 Timothy 2:8).

16. **With humility:** "If my people, which are called by my name, shall humble themselves, and pray, and seek my face, and turn from their wicked ways; then will I hear from heaven, and will forgive their sin, and will heal their land" (2 Chronicles 7:14; see also 33:12).

17. **With truth:** "The Lord is nigh unto all them that call upon him, to all that call upon him in truth" (Psalm 145:18; see also John 4:24).

18. **With a sincere desire to be heard:** "Let thine ear now be attentive, and thine eyes open, that thou mayest hear the prayer of thy servant, which I pray before thee now, day and night, for the children of Israel thy servants, and confess the sins of the children of Israel, which we have sinned against thee: both I and my father's house have sinned" (Nehemiah 1:6; see also Psalm 17:1; 55:1; 61:1).

19. **With a desire to receive an answer:** "Hear, O LORD, when I cry with my voice: have mercy also upon me, and answer me" (Psalm 27:7; see also Psalm 102:2; 108:6, 143:1).

20. **With boldness:** "Let us therefore come boldly unto the throne of grace, that we may obtain mercy, and find grace to help in time of need" (Hebrews 4:16).

21. **With seriousness:** "Night and day praying exceedingly that we might see your face, and might perfect that which is lacking in your faith?" (1 Thessalonians 3:10; see also James 5:17).

22. **With great persistence:** "And he said, Let me go, for the day breaketh. And he said, I will not let thee go, except thou

bless me" (Genesis 32:26; see also Luke 11:9; 18:1–7).

23. **At all times:** "Now she that is a widow indeed, and desolate, trusteth in God, and continueth in supplications and prayers night and day" (1 Timothy 5:5).

24. **Without ceasing:** "Pray without ceasing" (1 Thessalonians 5:17).

25. **Without worry:** "Be careful for nothing; but in every thing by prayer and supplication with thanksgiving let your requests be made known unto God" (Philippians 4:6).

Some Good Things to Bring with You When You Pray

1. **Repentance:** "When thy people Israel be smitten down before the enemy, because they have sinned against thee, and shall turn again to thee, and confess thy name, and pray, and make supplication unto thee in this house" (1 Kings 8:33; see also Jeremiah 36:7).

2. **Confession:** "And it came to pass, when I heard these words, that I sat down and wept, and mourned certain days, and fasted, and prayed before the God of heaven" (Nehemiah 1:4; see also Nehemiah 1:7).

3. **Humility:** "And Abraham answered and said, Behold now, I have taken upon me to speak unto the Lord, which am but dust and ashes" (Genesis 18:27).

4. **Weeping:** "They shall come with weeping, and with supplications will I lead them: I will cause them to walk by the rivers of waters in a straight way, wherein they shall not stumble: for I am a father to Israel, and Ephraim is my firstborn" (Jeremiah 31:9; see also Hosea 12:4).

5. **Fasting:** "And it came to pass, when I heard these words, that I sat down and wept, and mourned certain days, and fasted, and prayed before the God of heaven" (Nehemiah 1:4; see also Daniel 9:3; Acts 13:3).

6. **Watchfulness:** "But the end of all things is at hand: be ye therefore sober, and watch unto prayer" (1 Peter 4:7; see also Luke 21:36).

7. **Praise:** "I cried unto him with my mouth, and he was extolled with my tongue" (Psalm 66:17).

8. **Thanksgiving:** "Be careful for nothing; but in every thing by prayer and supplication with thanksgiving let your

requests be made known unto God (Philippians 4:6; see also Colossians 4:2).

9. **Persistence:** "I say unto you, Though he will not rise and give him, because he is his friend, yet because of his importunity he will rise and give him as many as he needeth" (Luke 11:8).

12 CONDITIONS FOR ANSWERED PRAYER

1. **Seeking God:** "I sought the LORD, and he heard me, and delivered me from all my fears" (Psalm 34:4).

2. **Seek God with all the heart:** "Then shall ye call upon me, and ye shall go and pray unto me, and I will hearken unto you. And ye shall seek me, and find me, when ye shall search for me with all your heart" (Jeremiah 29:12–13).

3. **Waiting on God:** "I waited patiently for the LORD; and he inclined unto me, and heard my cry" (Psalm 40:1).

4. **Returning to God:** "If my people, which are called by my name, shall humble themselves, and pray, and seek my face, and turn from their wicked ways; then will I hear from heaven, and will forgive their sin, and will heal their land" (2 Chronicles 7:14).

5. **Asking in faith:** "And the prayer of

faith shall save the sick, and the Lord shall raise him up; and if he have committed sins, they shall be forgiven him" (James 5:15).

6. **Asking in Christ's name:** "And whatsoever ye shall ask in my name, that will I do, that the Father may be glorified in the Son" (John 14:13).

7. **Asking in agreement with God's will:** "And this is the confidence that we have in him, that, if we ask any thing according to his will, he heareth us" (1 John 5:14).

8. **Fearing God:** "He will fulfil the desire of them that fear him: he also will hear their cry, and will save them" (Psalm 145:19).

9. **Keeping God's Commandments:** "And whatsoever we ask, we receive of him, because we keep his commandments, and do those things that are pleasing in his sight" (1 John 3:22).

10. **Abiding (remaining) in Christ:** "If ye abide in me, and my words abide in you, ye shall ask what ye will, and it shall be done unto you" (John 15:7).

11. **Being humble:** "If my people, which are called by my name, shall humble themselves, and pray, and seek my face,

and turn from their wicked ways; then will I hear from heaven, and will forgive their sin, and will heal their land" (2 Chronicles 7:14; see also Psalm 9:12).

12. **Living in righteousness:** "Confess your faults one to another, and pray one for another, that ye may be healed. The effectual fervent prayer of a righteous man availeth much" (James 5:16; see also Psalm 34:15).

22 Great Biblical Promises about Prayer

1. **"If my people, which are called by my name, shall humble themselves, and pray, and seek my face, and turn from their wicked ways;** then will I hear from heaven, and will forgive their sin, and will heal their land" (2 Chronicles 7:14).

2. **"The Lord is nigh unto all them that call upon him, to all that call upon him in truth.** He will fulfil the desire of them that fear him: he also will hear their cry, and will save them" (Psalm 145:18–19).

3. **"The sacrifice of the wicked is an abomination to the Lord:** but the prayer of the upright is his delight" (Proverbs 15:8).

4. **"And it shall come to pass, that before they call, I will answer;** and while they are yet speaking, I will hear" (Isaiah 65:24).

5. **"Call unto me, and I will answer thee,** and show thee great and mighty things, which thou knowest not" (Jeremiah 33:3).

6. **"And all things, whatsoever ye shall ask in prayer,** believing, ye shall receive" (Matthew 21:22).

7. **"Be not ye therefore like unto them:** for your Father knoweth what things ye have need of, before ye ask him" (Matthew 6:8).

8. **"Ask, and it shall be given you;** seek, and ye shall find; knock, and it shall be opened unto you" (Matthew 7:7; Luke 11:9).

9. **"If ye then, being evil, know how to give good gifts unto your children,** how much more shall your Father which is in heaven give good things to them that ask him?" (Matthew 7:11; see also Luke 11:13).

10. **"Again I say unto you,** That if two of you shall agree on earth as touching any thing that they shall ask, it shall be done for them of my Father which is in heaven" (Matthew 18:19).

11. **"Therefore I say unto you,** What things soever ye desire, when ye pray, believe that ye receive them, and ye shall have them" (Mark 11:24).

12. **"But I know,** that even now, whatsoever thou wilt ask of God, God will give it thee" (John 11:22).

13. **"And whatsoever ye shall ask in my name,** that will I do, that the Father may be glorified in the Son" (John 14:13).

14. **"If ye shall ask any thing in my name,** I will do it" (John 14:14).

15. **"If ye abide in me,** and my words abide in you, ye shall ask what ye will, and it shall be done unto you" (John 15:7).

16. **"Ye have not chosen me,** but I have chosen you, and ordained you, that ye should go and bring forth fruit, and that your fruit should remain: that whatsoever ye shall ask of the Father in my name, he may give it you" (John 15:16).

17. **"And in that day ye shall ask me nothing.** Verily, verily, I say unto you, Whatsoever ye shall ask the Father in my name, he will give it you" (John 16:23).

18. **"Hitherto have ye asked nothing in my name:** ask, and ye shall receive, that your joy may be full" (John 16:24).

19. **"Likewise the Spirit also helpeth our infirmities:** for we know not what we should pray for as we ought: but the Spirit itself maketh intercession for us with groanings which cannot be uttered" (Romans 8:26).

20. **"For the eyes of the Lord are over the righteous,** and his ears are open unto their prayers" (1 Peter 3:12).

21. **"And this is the confidence that we have in him,** that, if we ask any thing according to his will, he heareth us" (1 John 5:14).

22. **"And if we know that he hear us, whatsoever we ask,** we know that we have the petitions that we desired of him" (1 John 5:15).

PRAYER—IN PRIVATE AND IN PUBLIC

The Bible clearly teaches that God's people should get alone with God in a private place to pray (see Matthew 6:6, for example). Yet the same Bible extols the virtues of public prayer among God's people. Here are biblical examples of both:

20 Biblical Examples of Private Prayer

1. **Jesus** (Matthew 14:23; 26:36; 26:39)
2. **Lot** (Genesis 19:20)
3. **Abraham's servant** (Genesis 24:9–12)
4. **Jacob** (Genesis 32:9–12)
5. **Gideon** (Judges 6:22, 36, 39)
6. **Hannah** (1 Samuel 1:9–10)
7. **David** (2 Samuel 7:18–29)
8. **Hezekiah** (2 Kings 20:1–3)
9. **Isaiah** (2 Kings 20:11)
10. **Manasseh** (2 Chronicles 33:18–19)
11. **Ezra** (Ezra 9:5–6)
12. **Nehemiah** (Nehemiah 2:4)
13. **Jeremiah** (Jeremiah 32:16–25)
14. **Daniel** (Daniel 9:3, 17)
15. **Jonah** (Jonah 2:1)
16. **Habakkuk** (Habakkuk 1:2)
17. **Anna** (Luke 2:36–37)
18. **Saul** (Acts 9:11)
19. **Peter** (Acts 9:40; 10:9)
20. **Cornelius** (Acts 10:30)

Biblical Examples of Public Prayer

1. **Joshua** (Joshua 7:6–9)
2. **David** (1 Chronicles 29:10–19)
3. **Solomon** (2 Chronicles 6)
4. **Jehoshaphat** (2 Chronicles 20:5–13)
5. **The Levites** (Nehemiah 9)

6. **The Jews of Jesus' time** (Luke 1:10)
7. **First-generation Christians** (Acts 2:46; 4:24; 12:5; 12:12)
8. **Peter and John** (Acts 3:1)
9. **Teachers and prophets at Antioch** (Acts 13:1–3)
10. **The apostle Paul** (Acts 16:16)

30 IMPORTANT PRAYERS (SEE TEXT OF FIRST 20 IN CHAPTER 5)

1. **Abraham's bargaining for Sodom** (Genesis 18:16–33)
2. **Jacob's prayer for Esau's mercy** (Genesis 32:6–12)
3. **Jacob's prayer for blessing at Peniel** (Genesis 32:24–30)
4. **Moses' prayer at the burning bush** (Exodus 3:1–4:18)
5. **Moses' confession for Israel in the wilderness** (Exodus 32:9–14)
6. **Moses' plea for God's presence** (Exodus 33:12–34:9)
7. **Joshua's prayer after defeat at Ai** (Joshua 7:6–15)
8. **Hannah's prayer for a child** (1 Samuel 1:9–11)
9. **David's prayer when he was denied the privilege of building the temple** (2 Samuel 7:18–29)

10. **Solomon's request for wisdom**
    (1 Kings 3:4–10)
11. **Solomon's temple dedication prayer**
    (1 Kings 8:22–61)
12. **Hezekiah's petitions for Judah's
    deliverance** (2 Kings 19:14–19)
13. **Hezekiah's plea for his life** (2 Kings
    20:1–3)
14. **Ezra's confession of his people's sins**
    (Ezra 9:5–15)
15. **Nehemiah's prayer for success**
    (Nehemiah 1:1–11)
16. **Job's contrite prayer** (Job 42:1–6)
17. **David's prayer for pardon and
    confession of sin** (Psalm 51)
18. **David's prayer for deliverance from
    evil men** (Psalm 140)
19. **Isaiah's prayer for mercy** (Isaiah 64:
    1–12)
20. **Daniel's confession on behalf of his
    people** (Daniel 9:1–19)
21. **Jonah's contrite prayer** (Jonah 2:1–9)
22. **Habakkuk's questioning prayer**
    (Habakkuk 1:1–2:1)
23. **Habakkuk's prayer of praise**
    (Habakkuk 3:1–19)
24. **Jesus' "High Priestly" prayer** (John 17)
25. **Jesus' prayer at Gethsemane** (Matthew
    26:36–42)

26. **Jesus' prayer for His enemies** (Luke 23:33–34)
27. **The prayer of the dying, penitent criminal** (Luke 23:40–42)
28. **The church's prayer for boldness** (Acts 4:19, 23–31)
29. **Stephen, as he was martyred** (Acts 7:59–60)
30. **Paul, for the Ephesians** (Ephesians 1:1, 15–23; 3:14–21)

55 BIBLICAL EXAMPLES OF ANSWERED PRAYER

1. **Cain, for protection from God** (Genesis 4:13–15)
2. **Abraham, for a son** (Genesis 15)
3. **Abraham, for Sodom** (Genesis 18:23–33)
4. **Abraham, for Ishmael** (Genesis 17:18–20)
5. **Abraham, for Abimelech** (Genesis 20:9, 17)
6. **Hagar, for deliverance** (Genesis 16:7–13)
7. **Abraham's servant, for guidance** (Genesis 24:12–52)
8. **Rebecca, concerning her pains in pregnancy** (Genesis 25:21–26)
9. **Jacob, for protection from Esau** (Genesis 32:9–32; 33:1–17)

10. **Moses, at the Red Sea** (Exodus 14:15–16)

11. **Moses, at the waters of Marah** (Exodus 15:22–25)

12. **Moses, at Mount Horeb** (Exodus 17:4–6)

13. **Moses, in battle with the Amalekites** (Exodus 17:8–14)

14. **Moses, when Israelites complained for meat** (Numbers 11:11–34)

15. **Moses, for Miriam's leprosy** (Numbers 12:10, 13–15)

16. **Moses, Aaron, and Samuel** (Psalm 99:6)

17. **The people of Israel, for freedom from bondage** (Exodus 2:23–25; 3:7–10; Acts 7:34)

18. **The people of Israel, for protection from Pharaoh's army** (Exodus 14:10–30)

19. **The people of Israel, for protection from the king of Mesopotamia** (Judges 3:8–9, 15)

20. **Ammon** (Judges 10:6–18; 11:1–33)

21. **The people of Israel for freedom from Babylonian bondage** (Nehemiah 9:1, 5, 27)

22. **Gideon, asking for a sign from God** (Judges 6:36–40)

23. **Manoah, asking about Samson** (Judges 13:8–9)

24. **Samson, asking for strength** (Judges 16:28–30)

25. **Hannah, asking to become a mother** (1 Samuel 1:9–20)

26. **David, asking whether Keilah would be delivered into his hands** (1 Samuel 23:10–12)

27. **David, asking about Ziklag** (1 Samuel 30:1–8)

28. **David, asking whether he should go into Judah after Saul's death** (2 Samuel 2:1)

29. **David, asking whether he should go to war against the Philistines** (2 Samuel 5:19–25)

30. **Solomon, asking for wisdom** (1 Kings 3:5–13)

31. **Elijah, when raising the widow's son from the dead** (1 Kings 17:10, 21–22)

32. **Elijah, asking for a sign from God regarding his sacrifice** (1 Kings 18:36–38)

33. **Elijah, asking for rain** (1 Kings 17:1; 18:1, 42–45)

34. **Elisha, leading against the Syrian army** (2 Kings 6:17–20)

35. **Jabez, asking for prosperity** (1 Chronicles 4:10)

36. **Abijah, for victory over Jeroboam** (2 Chronicles 13:3–18)

37. **Asa, for victory over Zerah**
    (2 Chronicles 14:8–15)
38. **The people of Judah** (2 Chronicles
    15:15)
39. **Jehoshaphat, for victory over the
    Canaanites** (2 Chronicles 18:31;
    20:6–27)
40. **Jehoahaz, for victory over Hazael**
    (2 Kings 13:4)
41. **Hezekiah and Isaiah, for deliverance
    from Sennacherib** (2 Kings 19:14–20;
    2 Chronicles 32:20–22)
42. **To save Hezekiah's life** (2 Kings 20:1–7)
43. **The Reubenites, for deliverance from
    the Hagarites** (1 Chronicles 5:18–20)
44. **Manasseh, for deliverance from the king
    of Babylon** (2 Chronicles 33:11–13)
45. **The Jews, returning from the
    captivity** (Ezra 8:21, 23)
46. **Ezekiel, to have the baking of his
    bread of affliction changed** (Ezekiel
    4:12–15)
47. **Daniel, for the interpretation of
    Nebuchadnezzar's dream** (Daniel 2:1,
    16–23)
48. **Daniel, interceding for the people**
    (Daniel 9:20–27)
49. **Daniel, in a vision** (Daniel 10:9–12)
50. **Zacharias, for a son** (Luke 1:13)

51. **The leper, for healing** (Matthew 8:2–3; Mark 1:40–43; Luke 5:12–13)
52. **The centurion, for his servant** (Matthew 8:5–13; Luke 7:3–10; John 4:50–51)
53. **Peter, asking that Tabitha (Dorcas) be restored to life** (Acts 9:40)
54. **The disciples, for Peter** (Acts 12:5–17)
55. **Paul, to be restored to health** (2 Chronicles 1:9–11)

BIBLICAL EXAMPLES OF PERSISTENT PRAYER

1. **Jacob, for God's blessing** (Genesis 32:24–30)
2. **Moses, for his people** (Exodus 33:12–16)
3. **Elijah, for confirmation of God's calling** (1 Kings 18:22–44)
4. **The two blind men of Jericho for healing** (Matthew 20:30–31; Mark 10:48; Luke 18:39)
5. **The non-Jewish, Syro-Phoenician woman, for her daughter's healing** (Matthew 15:22–28)
6. **The Roman centurion, for his servant's healing** (Matthew 8:5; Luke 7:2–9)

EXAMPLES OF PRAYER WITH FASTING (ABSTAINING FROM FOOD)

1. **Jesus** (Matthew 4:1–2)
2. **Moses** (Exodus 34:27–28; Deuteronomy 9:9, 18)
3. **Elijah** (1 Kings 19:8–9)
4. **The nation of Israel** (Judges 20:26; Ezra 8:21; Esther 4:3)
5. **The Ninevites** (Jonah 3:5–8)
6. **David** (2 Samuel 12:16; Psalm 109:24)
7. **Nehemiah** (Nehemiah 1:1, 4)
8. **Esther** (Esther 4:15–16)
9. **Daniel** (Daniel 9:2–3)
10. **Disciples of John the Baptist** (Matthew 9:14)
11. **Anna** (Luke 2:36–37)
12. **Cornelius** (Acts 10:30)
13. **The early Christians** (Acts 13:1–2)

2
The Biblical Pillars of Prayer
THE FIVE DIFFERENT WAYS GOD WANTS YOU TO PRAY TO HIM

There are literally hundreds of references to prayer throughout the Bible. But did you know not all prayers are the same? In the Bible, there are five basic types of prayer, all of which are equally important to God: praise/worship, confession/penitence, petition/supplication (also known as requests), thanksgiving, and intercession.

In this chapter, you can read what the Bible has to say about each of these types of prayer.

PILLAR 1: PRAISE/WORSHIP

The Bible is filled with prayers of praise and worship to God—especially in the book of Psalms. Praise and worship are basically how we humans relate to God by verbally giving Him the glory for His greatness, goodness, power, and other attributes that make Him God.

10 BIBLICAL THINGS TO KNOW ABOUT PRAISE/WORSHIP

1. **It is fitting to praise God because He is God** (Psalm 33:1; 147:1).

2. **It should be offered from the soul** (Psalm 103:1; 104:1, 35).

3. **It should be offered with the entire heart** (Psalm 9:1; 111:1; 138:1).

4. **It should be done with an upright heart** (Psalm 119:7).

5. **It should be done with the mouth** (Psalm 51:15; 63:3; 119:171).

6. **It should be done joyfully** (Psalm 63:5; 98:4).

7. **It should be done with gladness** (2 Chronicles 29:30; Jeremiah 33:11).

8. **It should be done with thankfulness** (1 Chronicles 16:4; Psalm 147:7).

9. **It should be done continually** (Psalm 35:28; 71:6).

10. **It should be offered throughout life** (Psalm 104:33).

BIBLICAL REASONS GOD IS WORTHY OF PRAISE/WORSHIP

1. **His majesty** (Psalm 93:1; 96:6)

2. **His glory** (Psalm 138:5; Ezekiel 3:12)

3. **His excellence** (Exodus 15:7; Psalm 148:13)

4. **His greatness** (1 Chronicles 16:25; Psalm 145:3)

5. **His holiness** (Exodus 15:11; Isaiah 6:3)

6. **His wisdom** (Daniel 2:20; Jude 1:25)

7. **His power** (Psalm 21:13)
8. **His goodness** (Psalm 107:8; 118:1; 136:1; Jeremiah 33:11)
9. **His mercy** (2 Chronicles 20:21; Psalm 89:1; 118:1–4; 136)
10. **His lovingkindness and truth** (Psalm 138:2)
11. **His faithfulness and truth** (Isaiah 25:1)
12. **His salvation** (Psalm 18:46; Isaiah 25:9; 61:10; Luke 1:68–69)
13. **His wonderful deeds and work** (Psalm 89:5; 150:2; Isaiah 25:1)
14. **His comfort** (Psalm 23:4; Isaiah 12:1)
15. **His judgment** (Psalm 101:1)
16. **His wise counsel** (Psalm 16:7; Jeremiah 32:19)
17. **His faithfulness in fulfilling His promises** (1 Kings 8:56)
18. **His willingness to pardon of sin** (Psalm 103:1–3; Hosea 14:2)
19. **His deliverance** (Psalm 40:1–3)
20. **His protection** (Psalm 28:7; 59:17)
21. **His answers to prayer** (Psalm 28:6; 118:21)
22. **His spiritual blessings** (Psalm 103:2; Ephesians 1:3)
23. **His temporal blessings** (Psalm 136:1, 25)

24. **His continuous blessings** (Psalm 68:19)

21 BIBLICAL EXAMPLES OF PRAISE AND WORSHIP

1. **Melchizedek** (Genesis 14:18–20)
2. **Moses and the Israelites** (Exodus 15:1–21)
3. **Miriam** (Exodus 15:21)
4. **Jethro** (Exodus 18:10)
5. **The Israelites** (1 Chronicles 16:36)
6. **David** (1 Chronicles 29:10–13; Psalm 119:164)
7. **Deborah** (Judges 5)
8. **Hannah** (1 Samuel 2:1–10)
9. **The priests and Levites** (Ezra 3:10–11)
10. **Ezra** (Nehemiah 8:6)
11. **King Hezekiah** (Isaiah 38:2, 19)
12. **Zacharias** (Luke 1:59, 62–64)
13. **The shepherds** (Luke 2:20)
14. **Simeon** (Luke 2:25, 27–28)
15. **Anna** (Luke 2:36–38)
16. **Multitudes** (Luke 18:43)
17. **Jesus' disciples** (Luke 19:37–38)
18. **The apostles** (Luke 24:50–53)
19. **The first converts** (Acts 2:44, 46–47)
20. **The lame man who was healed** (Acts 3:2, 6–8)
21. **Paul and Silas in prison** (Acts 16:25)

Biblical Terms for the Praise of God

1. **Fruit of the lips** (Hebrews 13:15)
2. **Voice of praise** (Psalm 66:8)
3. **Voice of triumph** (Psalm 47:1)
4. **Voice of melody** (Isaiah 51:3)
5. **Voice of a psalm** (Psalm 98:5)
6. **Garment of praise** (Isaiah 61:3)
7. **Sacrifice of praise** (Hebrews 13:15)
8. **Sacrifices of joy** (Psalm 27:6)
9. **Calves of the lips** (Hosea 14:2)

Confession/Penitence

One of God's attributes that is so worthy of our praise and worship is His willingness and desire to forgive our sins. The Bible teaches that in order to receive that forgiveness, we must come to God praying prayers of confession ("Yes, I did it") and penitence ("With Your power, I endeavor to stop doing it").

Biblical Things to Know about Confession/Penitence

1. **God requires it** (Leviticus 5:5; Hosea 5:15).
2. **The Bible strongly encourages it** (Joshua 7:19; Jeremiah 3:13; James 5:16).
3. **It is the key to receiving God's mercy and forgiveness** (Proverbs 28:13).

4. **It should include a request for forgiveness** (2 Samuel 24:10; Psalm 25:11; 51:1; Jeremiah 14:7–9, 20)
5. **It should be done in humility** (Isaiah 64:5–6).
6. **There should be sorrow for sin** (Psalm 38:18; Lamentations 1:20).
7. **It should include the abandonment of sin** (Proverbs 28:13).
8. **It may include some restitution** (Numbers 5:6–7).
9. **It should be full and unreserved** (Psalm 32:5; 51:3; 106:6).
10. **It is followed by God's pardon/ forgiveness** (Psalm 32:5; 1 John 1:9).

BIBLICAL EXAMPLES OF CONFESSION/PENITENCE

1. **Aaron** (Numbers 12:11)
2. **The Israelites** (Numbers 21:6–7; 1 Samuel 7:6; 12:1, 19)
3. **King Saul** (1 Samuel 15:24)
4. **King David** (2 Samuel 24:10; Psalm 51)
5. **Ezra** (Ezra 9:5–6)
6. **Nehemiah** (Nehemiah 1:6–7)
7. **Levites** (Nehemiah 9:4, 33–34)
8. **Job** (Job 7:20)
9. **Daniel** (Daniel 9:4)
10. **Peter** (Luke 5:8)
11. **The thief on the cross** (Luke 23:39–42)

Petition/Supplication (Also Known As Requests)

When we use the term "answered prayer," we are referring to the type of prayer called petitions or supplications—or, in more modern language, requests. This is the part of prayer where we ask God for something. God loves to hear and answer His people's prayers of petition and supplication. That is largely because these prayers demonstrate the kind of dependence that is so fitting a heavenly Father/child of God relationship.

10 Biblical Things to Know about Petitions/Supplications

1. **Faith is essential in receiving the answer you seek** (Mark 11:23–24; James 5:15).
2. **Supplications should be offered in accordance with God's known will** (1 John 5:14–15).
3. **Supplications should be offered with right motives** (James 4:3).
4. **We should not worry but instead offer prayers *and* supplications** (Philippians 4:6).
5. **We should wait on God for our answers** (Psalm 40:1).
6. **We should ask in Christ's name** (John 14:13).

7. **We should approach God and ask boldly** (Hebrews 4:16).
8. **Keeping God's commandments is necessary for an answer** (1 John 3:22).
9. **We need to remain in Christ** (John 15:7).
10. **We should live in righteousness if we want God to grant our requests** (James 5:16; Psalm 34:15).

15 REASONS SUPPLICATIONS/PETITIONS ARE NOT GRANTED

1. **Unbelief** (James 1:6–8)
2. **Asking with wrong motivation/ selfishness** (James 4:3)
3. **Harboring sinful attitudes/actions** (Psalm 66:18)
4. **Unconfessed sin** (Isaiah 59:1–2)
5. **Offering unworthy service to God** (Malachi 1:7–9)
6. **Wandering away from God** (Jeremiah 14:10)
7. **Ignoring the call of God** (Proverbs 1:24–25)
8. **Not hearing the law of God** (Proverbs 28:9)
9. **Ignoring the plight of the poor** (Proverbs 21:13)
10. **Idolatry in the heart** (Ezekiel 14:3; see also Jeremiah 11:11–14)

11. **Wavering in faith** (James 1:6–7)
12. **Hypocrisy** (Job 27:8–9)
13. **Pride** (Job 35:12–13)
14. **Self-righteousness** (Luke 18:11–12, 14)
15. **Lack of persistence** (1 Thessalonians 5:17)

BIBLICAL EXAMPLES OF GRANTED SUPPLICATIONS/ PETITIONS

1. **Abraham** (Genesis 17:18, 20)
2. **Lot** (Genesis 19:18–21)
3. **Abraham's servant** (Genesis 24:15–27)
4. **Jacob** (Genesis 32:24–30)
5. **Israelites** (Exodus 2:23–24)
6. **Moses** (Exodus 17:4–6, 11–13)
7. **Samson** (Judges 15:16, 18–19)
8. **Hannah** (1 Samuel 1:22, 27)
9. **Samuel** (1 Samuel 7:9)
10. **Solomon** (1 Kings 3:6, 9–12)
11. **Man of God** (1 Kings 13:1, 6)
12. **Elijah** (1 Kings 18:36–38)
13. **Elisha** (2 Kings 4:32–35)
14. **Jehoahaz** (2 Kings 13:4)
15. **Hezekiah** (2 Kings 19:20)
16. **Jabez** (1 Chronicles 4:10)
17. **Asa** (2 Chronicles 14:11–12)
18. **Jehoshaphat** (2 Chronicles 20:5–17)
19. **Manasseh** (2 Chronicles 33:10–13, 19)
20. **Ezra** (Ezra 8:21–23)

21. **Nehemiah** (Nehemiah 4:9, 15)
22. **Job** (Job 42:10)
23. **David** (Psalm 18:6)
24. **Jeremiah** (Lamentations 3:55–56)
25. **Daniel** (Daniel 9:20–23)
26. **Jonah** (Jonah 2:2, 10)
27. **Zacharias** (Luke 1:13)
28. **Blind man** (Luke 18:35–43)
29. **Thief on the cross** (Luke 23:39–43)
30. **Apostles** (Acts 4:29–31)
31. **Cornelius** (Acts 10:1–4, 31)
32. **The early Christians** (Acts 12:5, 7)
33. **Paul and Silas** (Acts 16:25–26)

THANKSGIVING

God loves to answer His people's prayers, but He also loves to hear their words of appreciation for everything He has done for them. That includes the spiritual/heavenly blessings as well as the earthly/temporal ones.

10 BIBLICAL THINGS TO KNOW ABOUT THANKSGIVING

1. **The Bible commands it** (Psalm 50:14; Philippians 4:6).
2. **It should be offered regularly to God** (Psalm 50:14).
3. **It should be offered to Christ** (1 Timothy 1:12).

4. **It is to be offered through Christ** (Romans 1:8; Colossians 3:17; Hebrews 13:8, 15).
5. **It should be offered in private worship** (Daniel 6:10).
6. **It should be offered in public worship** (Psalm 35:18).
7. **It should be offered before meals** (John 6:11; Acts 27:35).
8. **It should be offered continuously** (Ephesians 1:16; 5:20; 1 Thessalonians 1:2).
9. **It should be offered for God's goodness and mercy** (Psalm 106:1; 107:1; 136:1–3).
10. **It should be part of prayer** (Philippians 4:6; Colossians 4:2).

11 THINGS TO BE THANKFUL FOR

1. **Christ's power** (Revelation 11:17)
2. **Freedom of sin through Christ** (Romans 7:23–25)
3. **The defeat of death** (1 Corinthians 15:55–57)
4. **The gift of wisdom** (Daniel 2:23)
5. **Converts** (Romans 6:17)
6. **The faith of others** (Romans 1:8; 2 Thessalonians 1:3)
7. **The love of others** (2 Thessalonians 1:3)

8. **God's grace on others** (1 Corinthians 1:4; Philippians 1:3–5; Colossians 1:3–7)
9. **God's nearness** (Psalm 75:1)
10. **God's provision for our needs** (Romans 14:6–7; 1 Timothy 4:3–4)
11. **Everything** (Ephesians 5:20)

BIBLICAL EXAMPLES OF THANKSGIVING

1. **David** (1 Chronicles 29:10, 13)
2. **Levites** (2 Chronicles 5:12–13)
3. **Daniel** (Daniel 2:20, 23)
4. **Jonah** (Jonah 2:1, 9)
5. **Simeon** (Luke 2:25–30)
6. **Anna** (Luke 2:36–38)
7. **Jesus** (Matthew 11:25; 26:26–27; John 6:11; 11:41)
8. **The apostle Paul** (Acts 28:15)

INTERCESSION

"Will you pray for me?" There may be no more honest, vulnerable question than this. When we show we are willing to pray for another, we draw closest to them—and to God—as we agree to petition Him to send that person His very best.

10 BIBLICAL THINGS TO KNOW ABOUT INTERCESSION

1. **It is commanded** (1 Timothy 2:1; James 5:14, 16).
2. **It is encouraged** (1 John 5:16).
3. **It is a sin to neglect it** (1 Samuel 12:23).
4. **It blesses the person praying** (Job 42:10).
5. **It is ineffective for the impenitent** (Jeremiah 7:13–16; 14:10–11).
6. **The Bible commands us to pray for all people** (1 Timothy 2:1).
7. **Jesus commanded His followers to pray for their enemies as well as for those who loved them** (Matthew 5:44).
8. **Jesus is our ultimate intercessor who still prays for us today** (Hebrews 7:22, 25).
9. **The word *intercession* literally means to "stand in the gap" for someone.**
10. **The apostle Paul encourages us to pray for all believers** (Ephesians 6:18).

PEOPLE/THINGS TO INTERCEDE FOR

1. **Those in authority** (1 Timothy 2:1–2)
2. **Ministers** (2 Corinthians 1:1, 11; Philippians 1:18–19)

3. **God's people/the Church** (Psalm 122:6; Isaiah 62:6–7; Ephesians 6:18)
4. **Children** (1 Samuel 1:27; Matthew 19:13)
5. **Friends** (Job 42:7–8)
6. **Fellow countrymen** (Romans 10:1)
7. **The sick** (James 5:14)
8. **Persecutors/enemies** (Matthew 5:44; Jeremiah 29:7)
9. **Those who forsake us** (2 Timothy 4:16)
10. **Those who complain against God** (Numbers 11:1; 14:19)
11. **By ministers for the people in their congregations** (Ephesians 1:16; 3:14–19; Philippians 1:4)

JESUS THE ULTIMATE INTERCESSOR

- **"But I have prayed for thee, that thy faith fail not:** and when thou art converted, strengthen thy brethren" (Luke 22:32).
- **"Then said Jesus, Father, forgive them; for they know not what they do.** And they parted his raiment, and cast lots" (Luke 23:34).
- **"I pray for them:** I pray not for the world, but for them which thou hast given me; for they are thine. And all

mine are thine, and thine are mine; and I am glorified in them. And now I am no more in the world, but these are in the world, and I come to thee. Holy Father, keep through thine own name those whom thou hast given me, that they may be one, as we are. While I was with them in the world, I kept them in thy name: those that thou gavest me I have kept, and none of them is lost, but the son of perdition; that the scripture might be fulfilled. And now come I to thee; and these things I speak in the world, that they might have my joy fulfilled in themselves (John 17:9–13).

- **"Wherefore he is able also to save them to the uttermost that come unto God by him,** seeing he ever liveth to make intercession for them (Hebrews 7:25).

18 BIBLICAL EXAMPLES OF INTERCESSION

1. **Abraham** (Genesis 18:23–32)
2. **Abraham's servant** (Genesis 24:12–14)
3. **Moses** (Exodus 8:12; 32:11–13)
4. **Samuel** (1 Samuel 7:5)
5. **King Solomon** (1 Kings 8:11, 30–36)
6. **Elisha** (2 Kings 4:32–33)
7. **King Hezekiah** (2 Chronicles 30:18)

8. **Isaiah** (2 Chronicles 32:20)
9. **Nehemiah** (Nehemiah 1:4–11)
10. **David** (Psalm 25:22)
11. **Ezekiel** (Ezekiel 9:8)
12. **Daniel** (Daniel 9:3–19)
13. **Stephen** (Acts 7:59–60)
14. **Peter and John** (Acts 8:14–15)
15. **Church of Jerusalem** (Acts 12:5)
16. **Paul** (Colossians 1:9–12;
    2 Thessalonians 1:11)
17. **Epaphras** (Colossians 4:12)
18. **Philemon** (Philemon 1:1, 22)

3

From the Saints of Old
SOME BIBLICAL PRAYERS TO REMEMBER

ABRAHAM'S BARGAINING WITH GOD FOR SODOM

And the men turned their faces from thence, and went toward Sodom: but Abraham stood yet before the LORD. And Abraham drew near, and said, Wilt thou also destroy the righteous with the wicked? Peradventure there be fifty righteous within the city: wilt thou also destroy and not spare the place for the fifty righteous that are therein? That be far from thee to do after this manner, to slay the righteous with the wicked: and that the righteous should be as the wicked, that be far from thee: Shall not the Judge of all the earth do right? And the LORD said, If I find in Sodom fifty righteous within the city, then I will spare all the place for their sakes. And Abraham answered and said, Behold now, I have taken upon me to speak unto the LORD, which am but dust and ashes: Peradventure there shall lack five of the fifty righteous: wilt thou destroy all the city for lack of five? And he said, If I find there forty and five, I will not destroy it. And he spake unto him yet again, and said, Peradventure there shall be forty found there. And he said, I will not do it for forty's sake. And he said unto him, Oh let not the LORD be angry, and I will speak: Peradventure there shall thirty be found there. And he said, I will not do it, if I find thirty there. And he said, Behold now, I have taken upon me to speak unto the LORD: Peradventure there shall be twenty found there. And he said, I will not destroy it for twenty's sake. And he said, Oh let not the LORD be angry, and I will speak yet but this once: Peradventure ten shall be found there. And he said, I will not destroy it for ten's sake.

Genesis 18:22–32

JACOB PRAYS FOR MERCY FROM ESAU

And the messengers returned to Jacob, saying, We came to thy brother Esau, and also he cometh to meet thee, and four hundred men with him.

Then Jacob was greatly afraid and distressed: and he divided the people that was with him, and the flocks, and herds, and the camels, into two bands; and said, If Esau come to the one company, and smite it, then the other company which is left shall escape. And Jacob said, O God of my father Abraham, and God of my father Isaac, the LORD which saidst unto me, Return unto thy country, and to thy kindred, and I will deal well with thee: I am not worthy of the least of all the mercies, and of all the truth, which thou hast shewed unto thy servant; for with my staff I passed over this Jordan; and now I am become two bands.

Deliver me, I pray thee, from the hand of my brother, from the hand of Esau: for I fear him, lest he will come and smite me, and the mother with the children. And thou saidst, I will surely do thee good, and make thy seed as the sand of the sea, which cannot be numbered for multitude.

Genesis 32:6–12

JACOB PRAYS FOR A BLESSING AT PENIEL

And Jacob was left alone; and there wrestled a man with him until the breaking of the day. And when he saw that he prevailed not against him, he touched the hollow of his thigh; and the hollow of Jacob's thigh was out of joint, as he wrestled with him. and he said, Let me go, for the day breaketh. And he said, I will not let thee go, except thou bless me.

And he said unto him, What is thy name? And he said, Jacob. And he said, Thy name shall be called no more Jacob, but Israel: for as a prince hast thou power with God and with men, and hast prevailed.

And Jacob asked him, and said, Tell me, I pray thee, thy name. And he said, Wherefore is it that thou dost ask after my name? And he blessed him there. And Jacob called the name of the place Peniel: for I have seen God face to face, and my life is preserved.

Genesis 32:24–30

Moses' Prayer at the Burning Bush (Abridged)

He said, I am the God of thy father, the God of Abraham, the God of Isaac, and the God of Jacob. And Moses hid his face; for he was afraid to look upon God. And the Lord said, I have surely seen the affliction of my people which are in Egypt, and have heard their cry by reason of their taskmasters; for I know their sorrows; and I am come down to deliver them out of the hand of the Egyptians, and to bring them up out of that land unto a good land and a large, unto a land flowing with milk and honey. . . . Come now therefore, and I will send thee unto Pharaoh, that thou mayest bring forth my people the children of Israel out of Egypt.

And Moses said unto God, Who am I, that I should go unto Pharaoh, and that I should bring forth the children of Israel out of Egypt? And he said, Certainly I will be with thee; and this shall be a token unto thee, that I have sent thee: When thou hast brought forth the people out of Egypt, ye shall serve God upon this mountain.

And Moses said unto God, Behold, when I come unto the children of Israel, and shall say unto them, The God of your fathers hath sent me unto you; and they shall say to me, What is his name? what shall I say unto them? And God said unto Moses, I AM THAT I AM: and he said, Thus shalt thou say unto the children of Israel, I AM hath sent me unto you. And God said moreover unto Moses, Thus shalt thou say unto the children of Israel, the LORD God of your fathers, the God of Abraham, the God of Isaac, and the God of Jacob, hath sent me unto you: this is my name for ever, and this is my memorial unto all generations.

Go, and gather the elders of Israel together, and say unto them, The LORD God of your fathers, the God of Abraham, of Isaac, and of Jacob, appeared unto me, saying, I have surely visited you, and seen that which is done to you in Egypt: And I have said, I will bring you up out of the affliction of Egypt. . .unto a land flowing with milk and honey. . . .

And I am sure that the king of Egypt will not let you go, no, not by a mighty hand. And I will stretch out my hand, and smite Egypt with all my wonders which I will do in the midst thereof: and after that he will let you go.

And I will give this people favour in the sight of the Egyptians: and it shall come to pass, that, when ye go, ye shall not go empty.

But every woman shall borrow of her neighbour, and of her that sojourneth in her house, jewels of silver, and jewels of gold, and raiment: and ye shall put them upon your sons, and upon your daughters; and ye shall spoil the Egyptians.

And Moses answered and said, But, behold, they will not believe me, nor hearken unto my voice: for they will say, The Lord hath not appeared unto thee. And the Lord said unto him, What is that in thine hand? And he said, A rod. And he said, Cast it on the ground. And he cast it on the ground, and it became a serpent; and Moses fled from before it.

And the Lord said unto Moses, Put forth thine hand, and take it by the tail. And he put forth his hand, and caught it, and it became a rod in his hand: That they may believe that the Lord God of their fathers, the God of Abraham, the God of Isaac, and the God of Jacob, hath appeared unto thee.

And the Lord said furthermore unto him, Put now thine hand into thy bosom. And he put his hand into his bosom: and when he took it out, behold, his hand was leprous as snow. And he said, Put thine hand into thy bosom again. And he put his hand into his bosom again; and plucked it out of his bosom, and, behold, it was turned again as his other flesh.

And it shall come to pass, if they will not believe thee, neither hearken to the voice of the first sign, that they will believe the voice of the latter sign. And it shall come to pass, if they will not believe also these two signs, neither hearken unto thy voice, that thou shalt take of the water of the river, and pour it upon the dry land: and the water which thou takest out of the river shall become blood upon the dry land.

And Moses said unto the Lord, O my Lord, I am not eloquent, neither heretofore, nor since thou hast spoken unto thy servant: but I am slow of speech, and of a slow tongue.

And the Lord said unto him, Who hath made man's mouth? or who maketh the dumb, or deaf, or the seeing, or the blind? have not I the Lord? Now therefore go, and I will be with thy mouth, and teach thee what thou shalt say.

And he said, O my Lord, send, I pray thee, by the hand of him whom thou wilt send. And the anger of the Lord was kindled against Moses, and he said, Is not Aaron the Levite thy brother? I know that he can speak well. And also, behold, he cometh forth to meet thee: and when he seeth thee, he will be glad in his heart.

And thou shalt speak unto him, and put

words in his mouth: and I will be with thy mouth, and with his mouth, and will teach you what ye shall do. And he shall be thy spokesman unto the people: and he shall be, even he shall be to thee instead of a mouth, and thou shalt be to him instead of God.

Complete prayer found in Exodus 3:1–4:18

MOSES' CONFESSION FOR ISRAEL IN THE WILDERNESS

And the LORD said unto Moses, I have seen this people, and, behold, it is a stiffnecked people: Now therefore let me alone, that my wrath may wax hot against them, and that I may consume them: and I will make of thee a great nation.

And Moses besought the LORD his God, and said, LORD, why doth thy wrath wax hot against thy people, which thou hast brought forth out of the land of Egypt with great power, and with a mighty hand? Wherefore should the Egyptians speak, and say, For mischief did he bring them out, to slay them in the mountains, and to consume them from the face of the earth? Turn from thy fierce wrath, and repent of this evil against thy people. Remember Abraham, Isaac, and Israel, thy servants, to whom thou swarest by thine own self, and saidst unto them, I will multiply your seed as the stars of heaven, and all this land that I have spoken of will I give unto your seed, and they shall inherit it for ever.

And the LORD repented of the evil which he thought to do unto his people.

Exodus 32:9–14

MOSES' PLEA FOR GOD'S PRESENCE

And Moses said unto the LORD, See, thou sayest unto me, Bring up this people: and thou hast not let me know whom thou wilt send with me. Yet thou hast said, I know thee by name, and thou hast also found grace in my sight.

Now therefore, I pray thee, if I have found grace in thy sight, shew me now thy way, that I may know thee, that I may find grace in thy sight: and consider that this nation is thy people.

And he said, My presence shall go with thee, and I will give thee rest.

And he said unto him, If thy presence go not with me, carry us not up hence. For wherein shall it be known here that I and thy people have found grace in thy sight? is it not in that thou goest with us? so shall we be separated, I and thy people, from all the people that are upon the face of the earth.

And the LORD said unto Moses, I will do this thing also that thou hast spoken: for thou

hast found grace in my sight, and I know thee
by name.

Exodus 33:12–17

JOSHUA'S PRAYER AFTER DEFEAT AT AI

And Joshua rent his clothes, and fell to the
earth upon his face before the ark of the LORD
until the eventide, he and the elders of Israel,
and put dust upon their heads. And Joshua
said, Alas, O LORD God, wherefore hast thou at
all brought this people over Jordan, to deliver
us into the hand of the Amorites, to destroy us?
would to God we had been content, and dwelt
on the other side Jordan! O LORD, what shall
I say, when Israel turneth their backs before
their enemies! For the Canaanites and all the
inhabitants of the land shall hear of it, and shall
environ us round, and cut off our name from
the earth: and what wilt thou do unto thy great
name?

And the LORD said unto Joshua, Get thee up;
wherefore liest thou thus upon thy face? Israel
hath sinned, and they have also transgressed
my covenant which I commanded them: for
they have even taken of the accursed thing, and
have also stolen, and dissembled also, and they
have put it even among their own stuff. Therefore
the children of Israel could not stand before
their enemies, but turned their backs before their

enemies, because they were accursed: neither will I be with you any more, except ye destroy the accursed from among you.

Up, sanctify the people, and say, Sanctify yourselves against to morrow: for thus saith the LORD God of Israel, There is an accursed thing in the midst of thee, O Israel: thou canst not stand before thine enemies, until ye take away the accursed thing from among you. In the morning therefore ye shall be brought according to your tribes: and it shall be, that the tribe which the LORD taketh shall come according to the families thereof; and the family which the LORD shall take shall come by households; and the household which the LORD shall take shall come man by man.

And it shall be, that he that is taken with the accursed thing shall be burnt with fire, he and all that he hath: because he hath transgressed the covenant of the LORD, and because he hath wrought folly in Israel.

Joshua 7:6–15

HANNAH'S PRAYER FOR A CHILD

And she was in bitterness of soul, and prayed unto the LORD, and wept sore. And she vowed a vow, and said, O LORD of hosts, if thou wilt indeed look on the affliction of thine handmaid, and remember me, and not forget thine handmaid, but wilt give unto thine handmaid a man child, then I will give him unto the LORD all the days of his life, and there shall no razor come upon his head.

1 Samuel 1:10–11

SOLOMON'S REQUEST FOR WISDOM

And the king went to Gibeon to sacrifice there; for that was the great high place: a thousand burnt offerings did Solomon offer upon that altar. In Gibeon the LORD appeared to Solomon in a dream by night: and God said, Ask what I shall give thee.

And Solomon said, Thou hast shewed unto thy servant David my father great mercy, according as he walked before thee in truth, and in righteousness, and in uprightness of heart with thee; and thou hast kept for him this great kindness, that thou hast given him a son to sit on his throne, as it is this day. And now, O LORD my God, thou hast made thy servant king instead of David my father: and I am but a little child: I know not how to go out or come in. And thy servant is in the midst of thy people which thou hast chosen, a great people, that cannot be numbered nor counted for multitude.

Give therefore thy servant an understanding heart to judge thy people, that I may discern between good and bad: for who is able to judge this thy so great a people?

And the speech pleased the LORD, that Solomon had asked this thing.

And God said unto him, Because thou hast asked this thing, and hast not asked for thyself long life; neither hast asked riches for thyself, nor hast asked the life of thine enemies; but hast asked for thyself understanding to discern judgment; behold, I have done according to thy words: lo, I have given thee a wise and an understanding heart; so that there was none like thee before thee, neither after thee shall any arise like unto thee. And I have also given thee that which thou hast not asked, both riches, and honour: so that there shall not be any among the kings like unto thee all thy days.

And if thou wilt walk in my ways, to keep my statutes and my commandments, as thy father David did walk, then I will lengthen thy days.

1 Kings 3:4–14

HEZEKIAH'S PETITION FOR JUDAH'S DELIVERANCE

O LORD God of Israel, which dwellest between the cherubims, thou art the God, even thou alone, of all the kingdoms of the earth; thou hast made heaven and earth.

LORD, bow down thine ear, and hear:

open, LORD, thine eyes, and see: and hear the words of Sennacherib, which hath sent him to reproach the living God.

Of a truth, LORD, the kings of Assyria have destroyed the nations and their lands, and have cast their gods into the fire: for they were no gods, but the work of men's hands, wood and stone: therefore they have destroyed them.

Now therefore, O LORD our God, I beseech thee, save thou us out of his hand, that all the kingdoms of the earth may know that thou art the LORD God, even thou only.

2 Kings 19:15–19

HEZEKIAH'S PLEA FOR HIS LIFE

Then he turned his face to the wall, and prayed unto the LORD, saying, I beseech thee, O LORD, remember now how I have walked before thee in truth and with a perfect heart, and have done that which is good in thy sight.

2 Kings 20:2–3

EZRA'S CONFESSION OF HIS PEOPLE'S SINS

O my God, I am ashamed and blush to lift up my face to thee, my God: for our iniquities are increased over our head, and our trespass is grown up unto the heavens.

Since the days of our fathers have we been

in a great trespass unto this day; and for our iniquities have we, our kings, and our priests, been delivered into the hand of the kings of the lands, to the sword, to captivity, and to a spoil, and to confusion of face, as it is this day.

And now for a little space grace hath been shewed from the LORD our God, to leave us a remnant to escape, and to give us a nail in his holy place, that our God may lighten our eyes, and give us a little reviving in our bondage.

For we were bondmen; yet our God hath not forsaken us in our bondage, but hath extended mercy unto us in the sight of the kings of Persia, to give us a reviving, to set up the house of our God, and to repair the desolations thereof, and to give us a wall in Judah and in Jerusalem.

And now, O our God, what shall we say after this? for we have forsaken thy commandments, which thou hast commanded by thy servants the prophets, saying, The land, unto which ye go to possess it, is an unclean land with the filthiness of the people of the lands, with their abominations, which have filled it from one end to another with their uncleanness.

Now therefore give not your daughters unto their sons, neither take their daughters unto your sons, nor seek their peace or their wealth for ever: that ye may be strong, and eat the good of the land, and leave it for an inheritance to your children for ever.

And after all that is come upon us for our evil deeds, and for our great trespass, seeing that thou our God hast punished us less than our iniquities deserve, and hast given us such deliverance as this; should we again break thy commandments, and join in affinity with the people of these abominations? wouldest not thou be angry with us till thou hadst consumed us, so that there should be no remnant nor escaping?

O LORD God of Israel, thou art righteous: for we remain yet escaped, as it is this day: behold, we are before thee in our trespasses: for we cannot stand before thee because of this.

Ezra 9:6–15

JOB'S PRAYER OF CONTRITION

Then Job answered the LORD, and said, I know that thou canst do every thing, and that no thought can be withholden from thee. Who is he that hideth counsel without knowledge? therefore have I uttered that I understood not; things too wonderful for me, which I knew not.

Hear, I beseech thee, and I will speak: I will demand of thee, and declare thou unto me. I have heard of thee by the hearing of the

ear: but now mine eye seeth thee. Wherefore I
abhor myself, and repent in dust and ashes.

Job 42:1–6

DAVID'S CONFESSION OF SIN AND PRAYER FOR PARDON

Have mercy upon me, O God, according
to thy lovingkindness: according unto the
multitude of thy tender mercies blot out my
transgressions. Wash me throughly from mine
iniquity, and cleanse me from my sin. For I
acknowledge my transgressions: and my sin is
ever before me.

Against thee, thee only, have I sinned, and
done this evil in thy sight: that thou mightest
be justified when thou speakest, and be clear
when thou judgest. Behold, I was shapen in
iniquity; and in sin did my mother conceive
me. Behold, thou desirest truth in the inward
parts: and in the hidden part thou shalt make
me to know wisdom.

Purge me with hyssop, and I shall be clean:
wash me, and I shall be whiter than snow.
Make me to hear joy and gladness; that the
bones which thou hast broken may rejoice.
Hide thy face from my sins, and blot out all
mine iniquities.

Create in me a clean heart, O God; and
renew a right spirit within me. Cast me not

away from thy presence; and take not thy holy spirit from me. Restore unto me the joy of thy salvation; and uphold me with thy free spirit.

Psalm 51:1–12

DAVID'S PRAYER FOR DELIVERANCE

Deliver me, O LORD, from the evil man: preserve me from the violent man; which imagine mischiefs in their heart; continually are they gathered together for war. They have sharpened their tongues like a serpent; adders' poison is under their lips. Selah.

Keep me, O LORD, from the hands of the wicked; preserve me from the violent man; who have purposed to overthrow my goings. The proud have hid a snare for me, and cords; they have spread a net by the wayside; they have set gins for me. Selah.

I said unto the LORD, Thou art my God: hear the voice of my supplications, O LORD. O GOD the Lord, the strength of my salvation, thou hast covered my head in the day of battle. Grant not, O LORD, the desires of the wicked: further not his wicked device; lest they exalt themselves. Selah.

As for the head of those that compass me about, let the mischief of their own lips cover them. Let burning coals fall upon them: let them be cast into the fire; into deep pits, that they rise not up again. Let not an evil speaker be established in the earth: evil shall hunt the violent man to overthrow him.

I know that the LORD will maintain the cause of the afflicted, and the right of the poor. Surely the righteous shall give thanks unto thy name: the upright shall dwell in thy presence.

Psalm 140

ISAIAH'S PRAYER FOR MERCY

Oh that thou wouldest rend the heavens, that thou wouldest come down, that the mountains might flow down at thy presence, as when the melting fire burneth, the fire causeth the waters to boil, to make thy name known to thine adversaries, that the nations may tremble at thy presence!

When thou didst terrible things which we looked not for, thou camest down, the mountains flowed down at thy presence. For since the beginning of the world men have not heard, nor perceived by the ear, neither hath the eye seen, O God, beside thee, what he hath prepared for him that waiteth for him.

Thou meetest him that rejoiceth and worketh righteousness, those that remember thee in thy ways: behold, thou art wroth; for we have sinned: in those is continuance, and we shall be saved.

But we are all as an unclean thing, and all our righteousnesses are as filthy rags; and we all do fade as a leaf; and our iniquities, like the wind, have taken us away. And there is none that calleth upon thy name, that stirreth up himself to take hold of thee: for thou hast hid thy face from us, and hast consumed us, because of our iniquities.

But now, O Lord, thou art our father; we are the clay, and thou our potter; and we all are the work of thy hand. Be not wroth very sore, O Lord, neither remember iniquity for ever: behold, see, we beseech thee, we are all thy people.

Thy holy cities are a wilderness, Zion is a wilderness, Jerusalem a desolation. Our holy and our beautiful house, where our fathers praised thee, is burned up with fire: and all our pleasant things are laid waste.

Wilt thou refrain thyself for these things, O Lord? wilt thou hold thy peace, and afflict us very sore?

Isaiah 64

DANIEL'S CONFESSION ON BEHALF OF HIS PEOPLE

And I set my face unto the Lord God, to seek by prayer and supplications, with fasting, and sackcloth, and ashes: And I prayed unto the Lord my God, and made my confession, and said, O Lord, the great and dreadful God, keeping the covenant and mercy to them that love him, and to them that keep his commandments; we have sinned, and have committed iniquity, and have done wickedly, and have rebelled, even by departing from thy precepts and from thy judgments: neither have we hearkened unto thy servants the prophets, which spake in thy name to our kings, our princes, and our fathers, and to all the people of the land.

O LORD, righteousness belongeth unto thee, but unto us confusion of faces, as at this day; to the men of Judah, and to the inhabitants of Jerusalem, and unto all Israel, that are near, and that are far off, through all the countries whither thou hast driven them, because of their trespass that they have trespassed against thee. O Lord, to us belongeth confusion of face, to our kings, to our princes, and to our fathers, because we have sinned against thee.

To the Lord our God belong mercies and forgivenesses, though we have rebelled against him; neither have we obeyed the voice of the LORD our God, to walk in his laws, which he set before us by his servants the prophets.

Yea, all Israel have transgressed thy law, even by departing, that they might not obey thy voice; therefore the curse is poured upon us, and the oath that is written in the law of Moses the servant of God, because we have sinned against him.

And he hath confirmed his words, which he spake against us, and against our judges that judged us, by bringing upon us a great evil: for under the whole heaven hath not been done as hath been done upon Jerusalem. As it is written in the law of Moses, all this evil is come upon us: yet made we not our prayer before the LORD our God, that we might turn from our iniquities, and understand thy truth.

Therefore hath the LORD watched upon the evil, and brought it upon us: for the LORD our God is righteous in all his works which he doeth: for we obeyed not his voice. And now, O Lord our God, that hast brought thy people forth out of the land of Egypt with a mighty hand, and hast gotten thee renown, as at this day; we have sinned, we have done wickedly.

O LORD, according to all thy righteousness, I beseech thee, let thine anger and thy fury be turned away from thy city Jerusalem, thy holy mountain: because for our sins, and for the iniquities of our fathers, Jerusalem and thy people are become a reproach to all that are about us. Now therefore, O our God, hear the prayer of thy servant, and his supplications, and cause thy face to shine upon thy sanctuary that is desolate, for the Lord's sake.

O my God, incline thine ear, and hear; open thine eyes, and behold our desolations, and the city which is called by thy name: for we do not present our supplications before thee for our righteousnesses, but for thy great mercies.

O Lord, hear; O Lord, forgive; O Lord, hearken and do; defer not, for thine own sake, O my God: for thy city and thy people are called by thy name.

Daniel 9:3–19

Jonah's Contrite Prayer

I cried by reason of mine affliction unto the Lord, and he heard me; out of the belly of hell cried I, and thou heardest my voice. For thou hadst cast me into the deep, in the midst of the seas; and the floods compassed me about: all thy billows and thy waves passed over me.

Then I said, I am cast out of thy sight; yet I will look again toward thy holy temple. The waters compassed me about, even to the soul: the depth closed me round about, the weeds were wrapped about my head.

I went down to the bottoms of the mountains; the earth with her bars was about me for ever: yet hast thou brought up my life from corruption, O Lord my God. When my soul fainted within me I remembered the LORD: and my prayer came in unto thee, into thine holy temple.

They that observe lying vanities forsake their own mercy. But I will sacrifice unto thee with the voice of thanksgiving; I will pay that that I have vowed. Salvation is of the LORD.

Jonah 2:2–9

HABAKKUK'S PRAYER QUESTIONING GOD

O LORD, how long shall I cry, and thou wilt not hear! even cry out unto thee of violence, and thou wilt not save! Why dost thou shew me iniquity, and cause me to behold grievance? for spoiling and violence are before me: and there are that raise up strife and contention.

Therefore the law is slacked, and judgment doth never go forth: for the wicked doth compass about the righteous; therefore wrong judgment proceedeth. Behold ye among the heathen, and regard, and wonder marvelously: for I will work a work in your days which ye will not believe, though it be told you.

For, lo, I raise up the Chaldeans, that bitter and hasty nation, which shall march through the breadth of the land, to possess the dwellingplaces that are not theirs. They are terrible and dreadful: their judgment and their dignity shall proceed of themselves. Their horses also are swifter than the leopards, and are more fierce than the evening wolves: and their horsemen shall spread themselves, and their horsemen shall come from far; they shall fly as the eagle that hasteth to eat. They shall come all for violence: their faces shall sup up as the east wind, and they shall gather the captivity as the sand. And they shall scoff at the kings, and the princes shall be a scorn unto them: they shall deride every strong hold; for they shall heap dust, and take it.

Then shall his mind change, and he shall pass over, and offend, imputing this his power unto his god. Art thou not from everlasting, O LORD my God, mine Holy One? we shall not die. O LORD, thou hast ordained them for judgment; and, O mighty God, thou hast established them for correction.

Thou art of purer eyes than to behold evil, and canst not look on iniquity: wherefore lookest thou upon them that deal treacherously, and holdest thy tongue when the wicked devoureth the man that is more righteous than he? And makest men as the fishes of the sea, as the creeping things, that have no ruler over them?

They take up all of them with the angle, they catch them in their net, and gather them in their drag: therefore they rejoice and are glad. Therefore they sacrifice unto their net, and burn incense unto their drag; because by them their portion is fat, and their meat plenteous. Shall they therefore empty their net, and not spare continually to slay the nations?

I will stand upon my watch, and set me upon the tower, and will watch to see what he will say unto me, and what I shall answer when I am reproved.

Habakkuk 1:2–2:1

HABAKKUK'S PRAYER OF PRAISE

O LORD, I have heard thy speech, and was afraid: O LORD, revive thy work in the midst of the years, in the midst of the years make known; in wrath remember mercy. God came from Teman, and the Holy One from mount Paran. Selah. His glory covered the heavens, and the earth was full of his praise. And his brightness was as the light; he had horns coming out of his hand: and there was the hiding of his power. Before him went the pestilence, and burning coals went forth at his feet.

He stood, and measured the earth: he beheld, and drove asunder the nations; and the everlasting mountains were scattered, the perpetual hills did bow: his ways are everlasting. I saw the tents of Cushan in affliction: and the curtains of the land of Midian did tremble.

Was the LORD displeased against the rivers? was thine anger against the rivers? was thy wrath against the sea, that thou didst ride upon thine horses and thy chariots of salvation? Thy bow was made quite naked, according to the oaths of the tribes, even thy word. Selah. Thou didst cleave the earth with rivers.

The mountains saw thee, and they trembled: the overflowing of the water passed by: the deep uttered his voice, and lifted up his hands on high.

The sun and moon stood still in their habitation: at the light of thine arrows they went, and at the shining of thy glittering spear. Thou didst march through the land in indignation, thou didst thresh the heathen in anger. Thou wentest forth for the salvation of thy people, even for salvation with thine anointed; thou woundedst the head out of the house of the wicked, by discovering the foundation unto the neck. Selah.

Thou didst strike through with his staves the head of his villages: they came out as a whirlwind to scatter me: their rejoicing was as to devour the poor secretly. Thou didst walk through the sea with thine horses, through the heap of great waters.

When I heard, my belly trembled; my

lips quivered at the voice: rottenness entered into my bones, and I trembled in myself, that I might rest in the day of trouble: when he cometh up unto the people, he will invade them with his troops.

Although the fig tree shall not blossom, neither shall fruit be in the vines; the labour of the olive shall fail, and the fields shall yield no meat; the flock shall be cut off from the fold, and there shall be no herd in the stalls: Yet I will rejoice in the LORD, I will joy in the God of my salvation.

The LORD God is my strength, and he will make my feet like hinds' feet, and he will make me to walk upon mine high places.

Habakkuk 3:2–19

JESUS' "HIGH PRIESTLY" PRAYER

See chapter 1, page 27

JESUS' PRAYER AT GETHSEMANE

See chapter 1, page 27
(Matthew 26:36–42)

THE CHURCH'S PRAYER FOR BOLDNESS

And when they heard that, they lifted up their voice to God with one accord, and said, Lord, thou art God, which hast made heaven, and earth, and the sea, and all that in them is: Who by the mouth of thy servant David hast said, Why did the heathen rage, and the people imagine vain things?

The kings of the earth stood up, and the rulers were gathered together against the Lord, and against his Christ. For of a truth against thy holy child Jesus, whom thou hast anointed, both Herod, and Pontius Pilate, with the Gentiles, and the people of Israel, were gathered together, for to do whatsoever thy hand and thy counsel determined before to be done.

And now, Lord, behold their threatenings: and grant unto thy servants, that with all boldness they may speak thy word, by stretching forth thine hand to heal; and that signs and wonders may be done by the name of thy holy child Jesus.

And when they had prayed, the place was shaken where they were assembled together; and they were all filled with the Holy Ghost, and they spake the word of God with boldness.

Acts 4:24–31

STEPHEN, AS HE WAS MARTYRED

And he kneeled down, and cried with a loud voice, Lord, lay not this sin to their charge. And when he had said this, he fell asleep

Acts 7:60

The Apostle Paul, for the Ephesians

Wherefore I also, after I heard of your faith in the Lord Jesus, and love unto all the saints, cease not to give thanks for you, making mention of you in my prayers; that the God of our Lord Jesus Christ, the Father of glory, may give unto you the spirit of wisdom and revelation in the knowledge of him: the eyes of your understanding being enlightened; that ye may know what is the hope of his calling, and what the riches of the glory of his inheritance in the saints, and what is the exceeding greatness of his power to us-ward who believe, according to the working of his mighty power, which he wrought in Christ, when he raised him from the dead, and set him at his own right hand in the heavenly places, far above all principality, and power, and might, and dominion, and every name that is named, not only in this world, but also in that which is to come: and hath put all things under his feet, and gave him to be the head over all things to the church, which is his body, the fulness of him that filleth all in all. . . .

For this cause I bow my knees unto the Father of our Lord Jesus Christ, of whom the whole family in heaven and earth is named, That he would grant you, according to the riches of his glory, to be strengthened with might by his Spirit in the inner man; that Christ may dwell in your hearts by faith; that ye, being rooted and grounded in love, may be able to comprehend with all saints what is the breadth, and length, and depth, and height; and to know the love of Christ, which passeth knowledge, that ye might be filled with all the fulness of God.

Now unto him that is able to do exceeding abundantly above all that we ask or think, according to the power that worketh in us, unto him be glory in the church by Christ Jesus throughout all ages, world without end. Amen.

Ephesians 1:15–23; 3:14–21

4
Jesus: The Ultimate Man of Prayer
CHRIST'S TEACHING AND EXAMPLE IN PRAYER

As the Son of God—God in "the flesh," as the Bible puts it—no one has ever had a better understanding of what prayer is, what it's for, and what it does than the Lord Jesus Christ. Jesus was completely and perfectly "in tune" with His heavenly Father, and He stayed that way through a life of perfect prayer.

Jesus prayed perfectly, and He also gave His followers the best teaching on prayer anyone has ever heard.

JESUS' TEACHINGS ON PRAYER

- **Pray for those who mistreat you:** "I say unto you, Love your enemies, bless them that curse you, do good to them that hate you, and pray for them which despitefully use you, and persecute you" (Matthew 5:44).
- **Don't pray in public so others will see you:** "And when thou prayest, thou shalt not be as the hypocrites are: for they love to pray standing in the synagogues and in the corners of the streets, that they may be seen of men.

Verily I say unto you, They have their reward" (Matthew 6:5).

- **Pray in private, knowing that God will reward you:** "But thou, when thou prayest, enter into thy closet, and when thou hast shut thy door, pray to thy Father which is in secret; and thy Father which seeth in secret shall reward thee openly" (Matthew 6:6).

- **Don't pray using repetition:** "But when ye pray, use not vain repetitions, as the heathen do: for they think that they shall be heard for their much speaking" (Matthew 6:7).

- **Pray knowing that God hears and knows what you need:** "Your Father knoweth what things ye have need of, before ye ask him" (Matthew 6:8).

- **The Model Prayer:** "After this manner therefore pray ye: Our Father which art in heaven, Hallowed be thy name. Thy kingdom come, Thy will be done in earth, as it is in heaven. Give us this day our daily bread. And forgive us our debts, as we forgive our debtors. And lead us not into temptation, but deliver us from evil: For thine is the kingdom, and the power, and the glory, for ever. Amen" (Matthew 6:9–13).

- **Pray that God will send workers out to win souls:** "Pray ye therefore the Lord of the harvest, that he will send forth labourers into his harvest" (Matthew 9:38).
- **Prayer and fasting are sometimes necessary in spiritual battle:** "Howbeit this kind goeth not out but by prayer and fasting" (Matthew 17:21, see also Mark 9:29).
- **Believing God is necessary for receiving from God:** "And all things, whatsoever ye shall ask in prayer, believing, ye shall receive" (Matthew 21:22).
- **Pray to fight temptation:** "Watch and pray, that ye enter not into temptation: the spirit indeed is willing, but the flesh is weak" (Matthew 26:41).
- **When you pray, forgive others:** "And when ye stand praying, forgive, if ye have ought against any: that your Father also which is in heaven may forgive you your trespasses" (Mark 11:25).
- **Jesus' own authority in prayer:** "Thinkest thou that I cannot now pray to my Father, and he shall presently give me more than twelve legions of angels?" (Matthew 26:53).

Jesus' Parables on Prayer

During His earthly ministry, Jesus often taught using parables—stories that made a point about the kingdom of God. Two of those parables dealt extensively with prayer and the part it would play in the disciples' lives—and in the lives of believers who followed them. The first, which is listed in Luke 18:1–8, deals with persistence in prayer, while the second, found in Luke 18:9–14, deals with the proper attitude of humility during prayer.

Parable of the Persistent Widow (Luke 18:1–8)

And he spake a parable unto them to this end, that men ought always to pray, and not to faint; saying, There was in a city a judge, which feared not God, neither regarded man: And there was a widow in that city; and she came unto him, saying, Avenge me of mine adversary.

And he would not for a while: but afterward he said within himself, Though I fear not God, nor regard man; yet because this widow troubleth me, I will avenge her, lest by her continual coming she weary me.

And the Lord said, Hear what the unjust judge saith. And shall not God avenge his own elect, which cry day and night unto him, though he bear long with them? I tell you that he will avenge them speedily. Nevertheless when the Son of man cometh, shall he find faith on the earth?

PARABLE OF THE PHARISEE AND THE TAX COLLECTOR (LUKE 18:9–14)

And he spake this parable unto certain which trusted in themselves that they were righteous, and despised others: Two men went up into the temple to pray; the one a Pharisee, and the other a publican. The Pharisee stood and prayed thus with himself, God, I thank thee, that I am not as other men are, extortioners, unjust, adulterers, or even as this publican. I fast twice in the week, I give tithes of all that I possess.

And the publican, standing afar off, would not lift up so much as his eyes unto heaven, but smote upon his breast, saying, God be merciful to me a sinner.

I tell you, this man went down to his house justified rather than the other: for every one that exalteth himself shall be abased; and he that humbleth himself shall be exalted.

More on the "Model Prayer," also known as "The Lord's Prayer"

Jesus didn't intend for His followers to simply recite what has come to be known as the "Lord's verbatim"; instead, He simply wanted them to remember this prayer so they could use it as a model for effective, life-changing interaction with God.

Here is the significance of the Lord's Prayer, line by line:

- **"Our Father which art in heaven":** This acknowledges God's true place while at the same time addressing Him as a personal heavenly Father.
- **"Hallowed be thy name":** This refers to the praise and worship that is due Him.
- **"Thy kingdom come, Thy will be done in earth, as it is in heaven":** This is a prayer of dependency and of submission to the will of God.
- **"Give us this day our daily bread":** We are to make our requests known to God and ask for daily provision.
- **"And forgive us our debts":** Confession of sin should be a part of any effective prayer to God.
- **"As we forgive our debtors":** It is important to God that His people

forgive one another for any wrongs
done.

- **"And lead us not into temptation,
  but deliver us from evil":** We are to
  pray for help in facing up to the trials
  and temptations that the devil and the
  world bring our way.

JESUS ALSO PRAYED FOR:

- **Children** (Matthew 19:13–14)
- **Himself and His mission on earth**
  (Matthew 26:36–44)
- **The apostle Peter** (Luke 22:31–32)
- **His disciples** (John 17:9–15)
- **Future believers** (John 17:20)
- **The coming of the Holy Spirit** (John
  16:25–27)

PLACES JESUS PRAYED

- **A mountain** (Matthew 14:23; Mark
  6:46; Luke 6:12)
- **The Mount of Transfiguration** (Luke
  9:28–36)
- **A "solitary place"** (Mark 1:35)
- **The Garden of Gethsemane** (Matthew
  26:36–45; Luke 22:41)
- **The wilderness** (Luke 5:16)

- **His prayer at Lazarus's tomb:** "Father, I thank thee that thou hast heard me. And I knew that thou hearest me always: but because of the people which stand by I said it, that they may believe that thou hast sent me" (John 11:41–42).

- "I thank thee, O Father, Lord of heaven and earth, because thou hast hid these things from the wise and prudent, and hast revealed them unto babes. Even so, Father: for so it seemed good in thy sight" (Matthew 11:25–26; see also Luke 10:21).

- **His prayer as his death approached:** "Now is my soul troubled; and what shall I say? Father, save me from this hour: but for this cause came I unto this hour. Father, glorify thy name" (John 12:27–28).

Jesus' High Priestly Prayer (John 17:1–26)

Jesus Prays for Himself

Father, the hour is come; glorify thy Son, that thy Son also may glorify thee: As thou hast given him power over all flesh, that he should give eternal life to as many as thou hast given him. And this is life eternal, that they might know thee the only true God, and Jesus Christ, whom thou hast sent.

I have glorified thee on the earth: I have finished the work which thou gavest me to do. And now, O Father, glorify thou me with thine own self with the glory which I had with thee before the world was.

Jesus Prays for His Disciples
I have manifested thy name unto the men which thou gavest me out of the world: thine they were, and thou gavest them me; and they have kept thy word. Now they have known that all things whatsoever thou hast given me are of thee.

For I have given unto them the words which thou gavest me; and they have received them, and have known surely that I came out from thee, and they have believed that thou didst send me. I pray for them: I pray not for the world, but for them which thou hast given me; for they are thine. And all mine are thine, and thine are mine; and I am glorified in them.

And now I am no more in the world, but these are in the world, and I come to thee. Holy Father, keep through thine own name those whom thou hast given me, that they may be one, as we are. While I was with them in the world, I kept them in thy name: those that thou gavest me I have kept, and none of them is lost, but the son of perdition; that the scripture might be fulfilled.

And now come I to thee; and these things I speak in the world, that they might have my joy fulfilled in themselves. I have given them thy word; and the world hath hated them, because they are not of the world, even as I am not of the world.

I pray not that thou shouldest take them out of the world, but that thou shouldest keep them from the evil. They are not of the world, even as I am not of the world. Sanctify them through thy truth: thy word is truth. As thou hast sent me into the world, even so have I also sent them into the world. And for their sakes I sanctify myself, that they also might be sanctified through the truth.

Jesus Prays for All Believers
Neither pray I for these alone, but for them also which shall believe on me through their word; that they all may be one; as thou, Father, art in me, and I in thee, that they also may be one in us: that the world may believe that thou hast sent me.

And the glory which thou gavest me I have given them; that they may be one, even as we are one: I in them, and thou in me, that they may be made perfect in one; and that the world may know that thou hast sent me, and hast loved them, as thou hast loved me.

Father, I will that they also, whom thou hast given me, be with me where I am; that they may behold my glory, which thou hast given me: for thou lovedst me before the foundation of the world.

O righteous Father, the world hath not known thee: but I have known thee, and these have known that thou hast sent me. And I have declared unto them thy name, and will declare it: that the love wherewith thou hast loved me may be in them, and I in them.

JESUS' PRAYERS AT GETHSEMANE

- "O my Father, if it be possible, let this cup pass from me: nevertheless not as I will, but as thou wilt" (Matthew 26:39).
- "O my Father, if this cup may not pass away from me, except I drink it, thy will be done" (Matthew 26:42).
- "Abba, Father, all things are possible unto thee; take away this cup from me: nevertheless not what I will, but what thou wilt" (Mark 14:36).
- "Father, if thou be willing, remove this cup from me: nevertheless not my will, but thine, be done" (Luke 22:42).

- "Father, forgive them; for they know not what they do" (Luke 23:34).
- "My God, my God, why hast thou forsaken me?" (Matthew 27:46; Mark 15:34).
- "It is finished" (John 19:30).
- "Father, into thy hands I commend my spirit" (Luke 23:46).

5
Some Great Sayings about Prayer
QUOTATIONS FROM PRAYING
MEN AND WOMEN

GENERAL QUOTATIONS

The purpose of prayer is to get God's will done.

Samuel Gordon
Quiet Talks on Prayer (1904)

I must pour out my heart in the language which His Spirit gives me; and more than that, I must trust in the Spirit to speak the unutterable groanings of my spirit, when my lips cannot actually express all the emotions of my heart.

Charles Spurgeon
"The Fatherhood of God" sermon (1858)

Every day you have another opportunity to affect your future with the words you speak to God.

Stormie Omartian
Just Enough Light for the Step I'm On (1999)

Sometimes a person prays with his tears, even when words are missing.

Bill Gothard
The Power of Crying Out (2002)

Daily prayer for daily needs.

E. M. Bounds
The Necessity of Prayer (19th century)

Faith thrives in an atmosphere of prayer.

E. M. Bounds
The Necessity of Prayer (19th century)

He prays not at all, who does not press his plea.

E. M. Bounds
The Necessity of Prayer (19th century)

Humility is an indispensable requisite of true prayer.

E. M. Bounds
The Essentials of Prayer (19th century)

Humility must be in the praying character as light is in the sun.

E. M. Bounds
The Essentials of Prayer (19th century)

Kneeling well becomes us as the attitude of prayer, because it betokens humility.

E. M. Bounds
The Essentials of Prayer (19th century)

What a nobility would come into life if secret prayer were not only an asking for some new sense of comfort, or light, or strength, but the giving a way of life just for one day into the sure and safe keeping of a mighty and faithful God.

Andrew Murray
The Prayer Life (1912)

Every day is a good day if you pray.

Norman Vincent Peale
The Power of Positive Thinking (1952)

When we feel least like praying is the time when we most need to pray.

R. A. Torrey
How to Pray (1900)

The prayer that is born of meditation upon the Word of God is the prayer that soars upward most easily to God's listening ear.

R. A. Torrey
How to Pray (1900)

There is no question God will duck, no battle He can't win, no topic He doesn't know. You can't make Him uncomfortable. You can't push Him too hard. So go ahead, hit Him with your best shot.

Karon Phillips Goodman
You're Late Again, Lord! (2002)

Unless the common course of our lives be according to the common spirit of our prayers, our prayers are so far from being real or sufficient degree of devotion that they become an empty lip-labor, or, what is worse, a notorious hypocrisy.

William Law
A Serious Call to a Devout and Holy Life (1729)

Let not the understanding, but the whole heart set upon the living God as the teacher, be the chief thing, when thou enterest thy closet. Then shalt thou find good understanding. God will give thee an understanding heart, a spiritual understanding.

Andrew Murray
Prayer's Inner Chamber (1912)

My prayers, my God, flow from what I am not; I think Thy answers make me what I am.

George MacDonald
Diary of an Old Soul (1880)

Look deep, yet deeper, in my heart, and there, beyond where I can feel, read thou the prayer.

George MacDonald
Diary of an Old Soul (1880)

Where I am most perplexed, it may be there
Thou mak'st a secret chamber, holy-dim, where
Thou wilt come to help my deepest prayer.

George MacDonald
Diary of an Old Soul (1880)

Remember, the shortest distance between
a problem and the solution is the distance
between our knees and the floor.

Charles Stanley
Handle with Prayer (1987)

Prayer allows a place for me to bring my
doubts and complaints and subject them to the
blinding light of reality I cannot comprehend
but can haltingly learn to trust.

Philip Yancey
Prayer: Does It Make Any Difference? (2006)

Most of us talk too much when we pray,
which is really kind of silly when you think
about it. If prayer is a conversation with God,
how can we hear what He has to say if we're
talking all the time?

Bob Buford
Game Plan (1997)

The benefits of prayer come not from praying but from living what we discover in prayer.

Matthew Kelly
A Call to Joy (1997)

When we can't pray, when the words won't come, when we don't know what to pray for, we have the Spirit within us, who prays for us. What an honor, what a privilege, what a gift. And what a God, who would make such provision for us!

Ray Pritchard
The God You Can Trust (2003)

Prayer is so universal and so natural that its place in our lives needs no defense. We all pray, and we pray because it is a part of our nature.

Robert and Debra Bruce
Reclaiming Intimacy (1996)

When people love one another, they pray for one another, and when they pray for one another, they learn to love one another more deeply.

Glenn Daman
Shepherding the Small Church (2002)

What we want is to press our case right up to the throne of God.

D. L. Moody
Prevailing Prayer: What Hinders It? (1884)

All true prayer must be offered in full submission to God.

D. L. Moody
Prevailing Prayer: What Hinders It? (1884)

To pray and not act is not only deception but also plain laziness.

Scott Hinkle
Recapturing the Primary Purpose (2005)

When we practice a rule of prayer, prayer gradually becomes a holy habit, something we do that is not dependent on feelings or moods or our ability to articulate well. It becomes central to our lives and strengthens our connections to God.

Valerie Hess and Marti Watson Garlett
Habits of a Child's Heart (2004)

If we are unwilling to change, we will abandon prayer as a noticeable characteristic of our lives.

Richard Foster
Celebration of Discipline (1978)

Fretting magnifies the *problem*, but prayer magnifies *God*.

Joanna Weaver
Having a Mary Heart in a Martha World (2000)

Prayer never evaporates.

Elisabeth Elliot
The Music of His Promises (2000)

Sometimes we need to pray about what to pray about.

Virginia Ann Froehle
Loving Yourself More (1993)

Prayer is not trying to manipulate God into doing our will.

Steve Campbell
"Foundations for Answered Prayer" sermon
(2009)

Not that you should imagine that the purpose of your prayer is to tell the Lord what you want; for He knows well enough what you need. Rather, the purpose of prayer is to make you ready and able to receive as a clean vessel the grace that our Lord would freely give to you.

Walter Hilton
Toward a Perfect Love (1985)

Every day as we have prayed, "Thy kingdom come," has our Christian consciousness taken in the tremendous sweep of that prayer and seen how it covers the length and breadth of this great world and every interest of human life?

Henry Drummond
A Life for a Life and Other Addresses
(1893)

When we pray more we can talk less.

A. W. Tozer "In Everything by Prayer"
sermon (20th century)

Ask God to open your heart and kindle in it a spark of His love, and then you will begin to understand what praying means.

Jean-Nicholas Grou
How to Pray (18th century)

Why do we pray so much with our lips and so little with our heart?

Jean-Nicholas Grou
How to Pray (18th century)

Prayer as Dependence upon God

True prayer is a spontaneous outpouring of honesty and need from the soul's foundation. In calm times, we say a prayer. In desperate times, we truly *pray*.

David Jeremiah
A Bend in the Road (2000)

True prayers are born of present trials and present needs.

E. M. Bounds
The Necessity of Prayer (19th century)

Prayer shows our dependence on God. It honors Him as the source of all blessing, and it reminds us that converting individuals and growing churches are His works, not ours.

Mark Dever and Paul Alexander
The Deliberate Church (2005)

Prayer is a declaration of our dependence on God. It isn't something mechanical you do; it is somewhere you go to meet Someone you know.

Jill Briscoe
The New Normal (2005)

The very thing that most qualifies us to pray is our helplessness.

> David Jeremiah
> *The Prayer Matrix* (2004)

Make no decision without prayer.

> Elizabeth George
> *A Woman after God's Own Heart* (1997)

Helplessness united with faith produces prayer.

> O. Hallesby
> *Prayer* (1931)

When all other courses of action have been eliminated, when we stand on the edge of the abyss, when we approach God with empty hands and an aching heart, then we draw close to the true heart of prayer.

> Jerry Sittser
> *When God Doesn't Answer Your Prayer* (2003)

The prayer of a Christian is not an attempt to force God's hand, but a humble acknowledgment of helplessness and dependence.

> J. I. Packer
> *Evangelism and the Sovereignty of God* (2008)

Prayers are needed. They are the winged messengers to carry the need to God.

John Wright Follette
Broken Bread (1957)

PRAYER AS COMMUNION WITH GOD

God knows what's in our hearts. We might as well get right to the point.

Bruce Bickel and Stan Jantz
God Is in the Small Stuff (1998)

In prayer man rises to heaven to dwell with God: in the Word God comes to dwell with man. In prayer man gives himself to God: in the Word God gives Himself to man.

Andrew Murray
The Prayer Life (1912)

The least little remembrance will always be acceptable to Him. You need not cry very loud.

Brother Lawrence
The Practice of the Presence of God (17th century)

Prayer provides nourishment for your soul, satiates that "inner" spiritual hunger, and helps you develop your relationship with a loving Father who can heal distraught relationships.

Robert and Debra Bruce
Reclaiming Intimacy (1996)

Most of us don't pray on a regular basis because we're aware it will cost us something. . . *honesty.*

Jack Hayford
Prayer Is Invading the Impossible (2002)

Prayer is not to get the goods. It is to enjoy the One who is good.

Jon Courson
Application Commentary (2003)

The great gift of God in prayer is Himself.

Maxie Dunnam
The Workbook of Intercessory Prayer (1979)

His prayer was nothing else but a sense of the presence of God.

Brother Lawrence
The Practice of the Presence of God (17th century)

To pray is to let Jesus into our lives.

O. Hallesby
Prayer (1931)

It is through prayer that we become friends with Christ.

Matthew Kelly
A Call to Joy (1997)

Thy praying voice is music in God's ears.

Matthew Henry
Commentary on the Whole Bible (1706)

I challenge you to shift the focus of your prayer. Don't spend a lot of time describing your mountain to the Lord. He knows what it is. Instead, focus your attention on the mountain mover—His glory, power, and faithfulness.

Bill Hybels
Too Busy Not to Pray (1988)

Prayer is our being in a constant state of understanding that we are in His presence, talking with Him as we would a friend—a father—and being ever intent on hearing His voice as He speaks to us.

Eva Marie Everson
Oasis (2007)

The call to unceasing prayer is not an invitation to divided consciousness; it does not imply that we pay any less attention to daily realities or retreat from life's responsibilities. . . [It] means being consciously constantly conscious of the presence of God amidst the changing complexion of everyday life.

Debra Farrington
Unceasing Prayer: A Beginner's Guide (2002)

The purpose of prayer is not primarily to move the hand of God but rather to hold the hand of God.

Jon Courson
Application Commentary (2006)

So many times we try to please God by the length of time we pray. Legislating prayer time becomes as unnatural as legislating conversations or hugs or kisses.

Steve Sampson
You Can Hear the Voice of God (1993)

Some people think God does not like to be troubled with our constant coming and asking. The only way to trouble God is not to come at all.

D. L. Moody
Prevailing Prayer: What Hinders It? (1884)

When we pray it is far more important to pray with a sense of the greatness of God than with a sense of the greatness of the problem.

Gordon Jackson
Destination Unknown (2004)

When the appointed times of prayer were past, he found no difference, because he still continued with God, praising and blessing Him with all his might, so that he passed his life in continual joy.

Brother Lawrence
The Practice of the Presence of God (17th century)

A little lifting up the heart suffices; a little remembrance of God, one act of inward worship, though upon a march, and sword in hand, are prayers which however short, are nevertheless very acceptable to God.

Brother Lawrence
The Practice of the Presence of God (17th century)

Prayer is related to our inborn hunger for God. And prayer is not for God's benefit, but for ours.

Robert and Debra Bruce
Reclaiming Intimacy (1996)

The heart has been poured out, and now lifted upon the wings of prayer the message is wafted up and away through the silent reaches of space to the Father's throne.

John Wright Follette
Broken Bread (1957)

Why do we not lay open our heart to God and beg Him to put into it whatever is most pleasing to Him?

Jean-Nicholas Grou
How to Pray (18th century)

The determined fixing of our will upon God, and pressing toward Him steadily and without deflection; this is the very center and the art of prayer.

Evelyn Underhill
The Essentials of Mysticism (1960)

Prayer, then, begins by an intellectual adjustment. By thinking of God earnestly and humbly to the exclusion of other objects of thought, by deliberately surrendering the mind to spiritual things, by preparing the consciousness for the inflow of new life.

Evelyn Underhill
The Essentials of Mysticism (1960)

An open life, an open hand, open upward, is the pipeline of communication between the heart of God and this poor befooled old world.

Samuel Gordon
Quiet Talks on Prayer (1904)

The essence of prayer is simply talking to God as you would to a beloved friend— without pretense or flippancy.

John MacArthur
Alone with God (1995)

I think of praying at all times as living in continual God-consciousness, where everything we see and experience becomes a kind of prayer, lived in deep awareness of and surrender to our heavenly Father.

John MacArthur
Alone with God (1995)

THE POWER OF PRAYER

Prayer and faith are sacred picklocks that can open secrets and obtain great treasures.

Charles Spurgeon
"The Holy Ghost—The Great Teacher" sermon (1855)

Prayer is the never-failing resort of the Christian in any case and in every plight.

Charles Spurgeon
"The Believer Sinking in the Mire" sermon (1865)

Prayer isn't getting your way in heaven; it's getting God's way on earth.

Greg Laurie
Wrestling with God (2003)

More can be accomplished in prayer in the first hours of the day than at any other time during the day.

R. A. Torrey
How to Pray (1900)

If we are to pray with power we must pray *with faith*.

> R. A. Torrey
> *How to Pray* (1900)

Nights of prayer to God are followed by days of power with men.

> R. A. Torrey
> *How to Pray* (1900)

God will use our simple prayers because of the authority behind them.

> Rich Mendola
> "The Acts of the Holy Spirit: Wonders and Good News" sermon (2009)

Prayer should be the means by which I, at all times, receive all that I need, and, for this reason, be my daily refuge, my daily consolation, my daily joy, my source of rich and inexhaustible joy in life.

> O. Hallesby
> *Prayer* (1931)

Someone has said that when we work, *we* work; but when we pray, *God* works. His supernatural strength is available to praying people who are convinced to the core of their beings that He can make a difference.

> Bill Hybels
> *Too Busy Not to Pray* (1988)

Scripture insists that God has hardwired the universe in such a way that He works primarily through prayer.

David Jeremiah
The Prayer Matrix (2004)

Prayer is the greatest power God has put into our hands for service—praying is harder work than doing, at least I find it so.

Mary Slessor
Mary Slessor of Calabar (1917)

Unless I had the spirit of prayer I could do nothing. If even for a day or an hour I lost the spirit of grace and supplication, I found myself unable to preach with power and efficiency, or to win souls by personal conversation.

Charles Finney
Memoirs of Rev. Charles G. Finney (1876)

The devil often laughs when we work, but he trembles when we pray.

Corrie ten Boom
Amazing Love (1953)

By praying more, we will not work any less, and we will accomplish vastly more.

R. A. Torrey
How to Bring Men to Christ (1893)

In your hour of desperation, where do you turn? Do you tell your troubles to anyone who will listen, or do you seek the throne of grace?

Michael Youssel
"A Prayer of Brokenness" (2009)

Prayer brings momentum. It lifts the heart above the challenges of life and gives it a view of God's resources of victory and hope.

John Mason
The Impossible Is Possible (2003)

Prayer may not change all things for you, but it sure changes you for all things.

John Mason
The Impossible Is Possible (2003)

More is accomplished by prayer than by anything else this world knows.

Ted Engstrom
Motivation to Last a Lifetime (1984)

Prayer is the preacher's mightiest weapon.

E. M. Bounds
Power Through Prayer (1906)

"In Everything by Prayer: An Unfailing Technique for Spiritual Success."

A. W. Tozer
sermon title (20th century)

For Christians prayer *is* like breathing.
You don't have to think to breathe because
the atmosphere exerts pressure on your lungs
and forces you to breathe. That's why it is
more difficult to hold your breath than it is
to breathe. Similarly, when you're born into
the family of God, you enter into a spiritual
atmosphere wherein God's presence and grace
exert pressure, or influence, on your life. Prayer
is the normal response to that pressure.

John MacArthur
Alone with God (1995)

ANSWERED AND UNANSWERED PRAYER

Tho' dark the way, still trust and pray,
The answering time will come.

Mary Wingate,
"The Answering Time Will Come" (1908)

God loves to hear and answer prayers. More
often than not, He is the God of "Yes."

Dave Earley
The 21 Most Effective Prayers of the Bible (2005)

Be sure to remember that nothing in
your daily life is so insignificant and so
inconsequential that the Lord will not help you
by answering your prayer.

O. Hallesby
Prayer (1931)

You thought God was to hear and answer you by making everything straight and pleasant—not so are nations or churches or men and women born; not so is character made. God is answering your prayer in His way.

Mary Slessor
Mary Slessor of Calabar (1917)

If we knock, God has promised to open the door and grant our request. It may be years before the answer comes; He may keep us knocking; but He has promised that the answer will come.

D. L. Moody
Prevailing Prayer: What Hinders It? (1884)

I ask Him daily and often momently to give me wisdom, understanding, and bodily strength to do His will; hence I am asking and receiving all the time.

George Washington Carver
George Washington Carver in His Own Words (1941)

We need to ask God to take this fragile, selfish, flawed self of ours and make it more like Him. God will answer that prayer.

Jerry Sittser
When God Doesn't Answer Your Prayer (2003)

I know what it is to pray long years and never get the answer—I had to pray for my father. But I know my heavenly Father so well I can leave it with Him for the lower fatherhood.

Mary Slessor
Mary Slessor of Calabar (1917)

Unanswered prayer never becomes a significant issue until we really need an answer to prayer, until our life depends on an answer. Then we cry out to God out of a deep sense of need. We pray out of desperation.

Jerry Sittser
When God Doesn't Answer Your Prayer (2003)

God detests the prayers of a man who has no delight in His Word. When we live with a closed Bible, we live with a closed heaven; God will not answer our prayers.

Charles Stanley
Handle with Prayer (1987)

No matter how intense or fervent or long your prayers may be, if you have unconfessed sin in your life, your prayers are really going nowhere.

Greg Laurie
Wrestling with God (2003)

The reason why we don't pray more—and probably don't see more answers to prayer—is not because we don't know how to pray but because we don't really need to pray. We are not desperate enough.

Jerry Sittser
When God Doesn't Answer Your Prayer (2003)

We are to ask with a beggar's humility, to seek with a servant's carefulness, and to knock with the confidence of a friend.

D. L. Moody
Prevailing Prayer: What Hinders It? (1884)

Be specific with God in prayer, and He will be specific with you in regard to the answer.

David Wilkerson
Prayer—The Long and Short of It! (2009)

We must have a warrant for our prayers. If we have some great desire, we must search the scriptures to find if it be right to ask it.

D. L. Moody
Prevailing Prayer: What Hinders It? (1884)

We cannot be too frequent in our requests; God will not weary of His children's prayers.

D. L. Moody
Prevailing Prayer: What Hinders It? (1884)

My life is one long daily, hourly record of answered prayer.

Mary Slessor
Mary Slessor of Calabar (1917)

There are more tears shed over answered prayers than over unanswered prayers.

Teresa of Avila
(16th century)

INTERCESSORY PRAYER

Have you ever learned the beautiful art of letting God take care of you and giving all your thought and strength to pray for others and for the kingdom of God? It will relieve you of a thousand cares.

A. B. Simpson
Days of Heaven Upon Earth (1897)

And that is the ultimate purpose of all this intercession: not just to save our own from the world, but to save the world through our own.

Agnes Sanford
The Healing Light (1947)

If we have our eyes and hearts open, there are many who need our prayers each day. Just reading the newspaper or watching the evening news provides ample opportunity for intercessory prayers—prayers on behalf of others.

Debra Farrington
A Beginner's Guide to Unceasing Prayer (2002)

When you pray for unconverted people, you do so on the assumption that it is in God's power to bring them to faith. You entreat Him to do that very thing, and your confidence in asking rests on the certainty that He is able to do what you ask.

J. I. Packer
Evangelism and the Sovereignty of God (2008)

When we hold up the life of another before God, when we expose it to God's love, when we pray. . .only then do we sense what it means to share in God's work, in His concern; only then do the walls that separate us from others go down and we sense that we are at bottom all knit together in a great and intimate family.

Douglas Steere
Prayer and Worship (1978)

There is no greater intimacy with another than that which is built through holding him or her up in prayer.

Douglas Steere
Prayer and Worship (1978)

Despite disappointments, the Christian is obligated to pray for the sick because we are bidden to do so and because the crumb of our caring is but a morsel broken from the whole loaf of the Father's infinite and tender love.

Catherine Marshall
Something More (1974)

Never stop praying for "hopeless" cases.

Robert Morgan
Moments for Families with Prodigals (2003)

Intercessory prayer is an extension of the ministry of Jesus through His Body, the Church, whereby we mediate between God and humanity for the purpose of reconciling the world to Him, or between Satan and humanity for the purpose of enforcing the victory of Calvary.

Dutch Sheets
Intercessory Prayer (1996)

There was a man convicted and converted in answer to prayer. So if you are anxious about the conversion of some relative, or some friend, make up your mind that you will give God no rest, day or night, till He grants your petition.

D. L. Moody
Prevailing Prayer: What Hinders It? (1884)

A "prayer warrior" is a person who is convinced that God is omnipotent—that God has the power to do anything, to change anyone, and to intervene in any circumstance. A person who truly believes this refuses to doubt God.

Bill Hybels
Too Busy Not to Pray (1988)

6
Some Prayers to Remember
Samples of Famous Prayers by Famous People

Prayers of Devotion to God

My Lord God, I have no idea where I am going. I do not see the road ahead of me. I cannot know for certain where it will end. Nor do I really know myself, and the fact that I think I am following Your will does not mean that I am actually doing so. But I believe that the desire to please You does in fact please You. And I hope that I have that desire in all that I am doing. I hope that I will never do anything apart from that desire. And I know that if I do this You will lead me by the right road though I may know nothing about it. Therefore will I trust You always though I may seem to be lost and in the shadow of death. I will not fear, for You are ever with me, and will never leave me to face my perils alone.

Thomas Merton (1915–1968)

My God, I love Thee; not because
I hope for Heav'n thereby,
Nor yet because who love Thee not
May eternally die.

Thou, O my Jesus, Thou didst me
Upon the cross embrace;
For me didst bear the nails and spear,
And manifold disgrace.

And griefs and torments numberless,
And sweat of agony;
E'en death itself; and all for man
Who was Thine enemy.

Then why, O blessed Jesus Christ
Should I not love Thee well?
Not for the hope of winning heaven,
Nor of escaping hell.

Not with the hope of gaining aught,
Nor seeking a reward,
But as Thyself hast loved me,
O everlasting Lord!

E'en so I love Thee, and will love,
And in Thy praise will sing,
Solely because Thou art my God,
And my eternal King.

  Attributed to Francis Xavier (1506–1552)

What shall I give You, Lord, in return for all
Your kindness?
  Glory to You for Your love.
  Glory to You for Your mercy.
  Glory to You for Your patience.

Glory to You for forgiving us all our sins.

Glory to You for coming to save our souls.

Glory to You for Your incarnation in the
virgin's womb.

Glory to You for Your bonds.

Glory to You for receiving the cut of the
lash.

Glory to You for accepting mockery.

Glory to You for Your crucifixion.

Glory to You for Your burial.

Glory to You for Your resurrection.

Glory to You who as preached to men and
women.

Glory to You in whom they believed.

Glory to You who was taken up into
heaven.

Glory to You who sits in the great glory at
the Father's right hand.

Glory to You whose will it is that the sinner
should be saved through Your great
mercy and compassion.

Ephraem of Syria (c. 306–373)

Thanks be to You, our Lord Jesus Christ,
for all the benefits which You have given us,
for all the pains and insults which You have
borne for us. Most merciful Redeemer, Friend
and Brother, may we know You more clearly,
love You more dearly, and follow You more
nearly, day by day.

Richard of Chichester (1197–1253)

Almighty God, in whom we live and move and have our being, who hast made us for Thyself, so that our hearts are restless till they rest in Thee: Grant us purity of heart and strength of purpose, that no selfish passion may hinder us from knowing Thy will, no weakness from doing it; but that in Thy light we may see light clearly, and in Thy service find our perfect freedom; through Jesus Christ our Lord.

Augustine of Hippo (345–430)

The Serenity Prayer

God grant me the serenity
To accept the things I cannot change;
Courage to change the things I can;
And wisdom to know the difference.
Living one day at a time;
Enjoying one moment at a time;
Accepting hardships as the pathway to peace;
Taking, as He did, this sinful world
As it is, not as I would have it;
Trusting that He will make all things right
If I surrender to His will;
So that I may be reasonably happy in this life
And supremely happy with Him
Forever and ever in the next.

Reinhold Niebuhr (1892–1971)

God of the day and of the night,
in me there is darkness,
but with You there is light.
I am alone, but You will not leave me.
I am weak, but You will come to my help.
I am restless, but You are my peace.
I am in haste, but You are the God
of infinite patience.
I am confused and lost,
but You are eternal wisdom
and You direct my path;
now and forever. Amen.
Dietrich Bonhoeffer (1906–1945)

St. Patrick's Breastplate

I arise today
Through a mighty strength,
the invocation of the Trinity,
Through the belief in the threeness,
Through confession of the oneness
Of the Creator of creation.

I arise today
Through the strength of Christ's birth
with His baptism,
Through the strength of His crucifixion with
His burial,
Through the strength of His resurrection with
His ascension,
Through the strength of His descent for the
judgment of doom.

I arise today
Through the strength of the love of cherubim,
In obedience of angels,
In the service of archangels,
In hope of resurrection to meet with reward,
In prayers of patriarchs,
In predictions of prophets,
In preaching of apostles,
In faith of confessors,
In innocence of holy virgins,
In deeds of righteous men.

I arise today
Through the strength of heaven:
Light of sun,
Radiance of moon,
Splendor of fire,
Speed of lightning,
Swiftness of wind,
Depth of sea,
Stability of earth,
Firmness of rock.

I arise today
Through God's strength to pilot me,
God's might to uphold me,
God's wisdom to guide me,
God's eye to look before me,
God's ear to hear me,
God's word to speak for me,
God's hand to guard me,

God's way to lie before me,
God's shield to protect me,
God's host to save me
From snares of devils,
From temptations of vices,
From everyone who shall wish me ill,
Afar and anear,
Alone and in multitude.

I summon today all these powers between me
and those evils,
Against every cruel merciless power that may
oppose my body and soul,
Against incantations of false prophets,
Against black laws of pagandom
Against false laws of heretics,
Against craft of idolatry,
Against spells of witches
and smiths and wizards,
Against every knowledge that corrupts
man's body and soul.
Christ to shield me today
Against poison, against burning,
Against drowning, against wounding,
So that there may come to me
abundance of reward.

Christ with me, Christ before me,
Christ behind me,
Christ in me, Christ beneath me,
Christ above me,

Christ on my right, Christ on my left,
Christ when I lie down, Christ when I sit
down, Christ when I arise,
Christ in the heart of every man
who thinks of me,
Christ in the mouth of everyone
who speaks of me,
Christ in every eye that sees me,
Christ in every ear that hears me.

I arise today
Through a mighty strength, the invocation of
the Trinity,
Through belief in the threeness,
Through confession of the oneness,
Of the Creator of creation.

St. Patrick of Ireland (387–493)

O Lord, teach me to seek You, and reveal
Yourself to me when I seek You. For I cannot
seek You unless You first teach me, nor find
You unless You first reveal Yourself to me. Let
me seek You in longing, and long for You in
seeking. Let me find You in love, and love You
in finding.

Ambrose of Milan (c. 340–397)

O Lord, who in infinite wisdom and
love orders all things for Your children, order
everything this day for me in Your tender pity.
You know my weakness, who made me; You

know how my soul shrinks from all pain of soul. Lord, I know You will lay no greater burden on me than You can help me to bear. Teach me to receive all things this day from You. Enable me to commend myself in all things to You; grant me in all things to please You; bring me through all things nearer to You; bring me, day by day, nearer to Yourself, to life everlasting. Amen.

Edward Bouverie Pusey (1800–1882)

PRAYERS OF COMMITMENT TO SERVICE

Prayer of St. Francis

Lord, make me an instrument of Your peace;
where there is hatred, let me sow love;
where there is injury, pardon;
where there is doubt, faith;
where there is despair, hope;
where there is darkness, light;
and where there is sadness, joy.

O divine Master,
grant that I may not so much seek to be
consoled as to console;
to be understood, as to understand;
to be loved, as to love;
for it is in giving that we receive,
it is in pardoning that we are pardoned,
and it is in dying that we are born to eternal life.

Francis of Assisi (1181–1226)

Strengthen us, our God, to relieve the oppressed, to hear the groans of poor prisoners, to reform the abuses from all professionals, that many be made not poor to make a few rich.

Oliver Cromwell (1599–1658)

God of love, we pray that You give us love: love in our thinking, love in our speaking, love in our doing, and love in the hidden places of our souls; love of our neighbors, near and far; love of our friends, old and new; love of those whom we find it hard to bear, and love of those who find it hard to bear with us; love of those with whom we work, and love of those with whom we take our ease; love in joy, love in sorrow; love in life and love in death; that so at length we may be worthy to dwell with You, who are eternal love, Father, Son, and Holy Spirit, forever and ever.

William Temple (1881–1944)

Lord when I am hungry,
give me someone needing food;
When I am thirsty,
send me someone needing a drink;
When I am cold, send me
someone to warm;
When I am grieved, send me
someone to console;
When my cross grows heavy
let me carry another's cross, too;

When I am poor, lend me
someone in need;
When I have no time,
give me someone I can help a little while;
When I am humiliated,
let me have someone to praise;
When I am disheartened,
send me someone to cheer;
When I need understanding,
give me someone who needs mine;
When I need to be looked after,
give me someone to care for;
When I think only of myself,
draw my thoughts to another.

Author Unknown

Lord, give us such a strong love for You as
may sweeten our obedience. Let us not serve
You with the spirit of bondage as slaves, but
with cheerfulness and gladness, rejoicing in Your
work.

Benjamin Jenks (1646–1724)

Teach us, good Lord, to serve You
as You deserve:
to give, and not to count the cost,
to fight, and not to heed the wounds,
to toil, and not to seek for rest,
to labor, and not to ask for any reward,
save that of knowing that we do Your will.

Ignatius of Loyola (1491–1556)

Dear Jesus, help us to spread your fragrance everywhere we go; flood our souls with Your Spirit and life. Penetrate and possess our whole being so utterly that our lives may only be a radiance of Yours. Shine through us and be so in us that every soul we come in contact with may feel Your presence in our soul. Let them look up and see no longer us but only Jesus. Stay with us and then we shall begin to shine as You shine, so to shine as to be light to others. The light, O Jesus, will be all from You. None of it will be ours. It will be Your shining on others through us. Let us thus praise You in the way You love best by shining on those around us. Let us preach You without preaching, not by words, but by our example, by the catching force the sympathetic influence of what we do, the evident fullness of the love our hearts bear to You.

Mother Teresa of Calcutta (1910–1997)

Lord, open my eyes that I may see the needs of others, open my ears that I may hear their cries, open my heart so that they need not be without relief. Let me not be afraid to defend the weak because of the anger of the strong, nor afraid to defend the poor because of the anger of the rich. Show me where love and hope and faith are needed, and use me to bring them to these places. Open my eyes and ears that I may, this coming day, be able to do some work of peace for You.

Alan Stewart Paton (1903–1988)

Use me, then, my Savior, for whatever
purpose and in whatever way You may require.
Here is my poor heart, an empty vessel. Fill it
with Your grace.

D. L. Moody (1837–1899)

Lord Jesus, bless all who serve us, who
have dedicated their lives to the ministry of
others—all the teachers of our schools who
labor so patiently with so little appreciation;
all who wait upon the public, the clerks
in the stores who have to accept criticism,
complaints, bad manners, and selfishness
at the hands of a thoughtless public. Bless
the mailman, the drivers of streetcars and
buses who must listen to people who lose
their tempers. Bless every humble soul who,
in these days of stress and strain, preaches
sermons without words. Amen.

Peter Marshall (1902–1949)

Make us worthy, Lord, to serve our fellow
men throughout the world who live and die in
poverty and hunger. Give them, through our
hands, this day their daily bread, and by our
understanding love, give peace and joy.

Mother Teresa of Calcutta (1910–1997)

Let us go forth
In the goodness of our merciful Father,
In the gentleness of our brother Jesus,
In the radiance of His Holy Spirit,
In the faith of the apostles,
In the joyful praise of the angels,
In the holiness of the saints,
In the courage of the martyrs.

Celtic Prayer

Hands who touched the leper, touch my
wounded heart;
Hands who healed the blind man, heal my
aching soul;
Hands who cured the lame, mend my
disjointed life;
Hands who embraced all life, enfold me in
Your peace.
Lord, merely touch and heal, cure and forgive.

This is my prayer to Thee, my Lord;
Give me strength lightly to bear my joys and
sorrows;
Give me the strength to make my love fruitful
in service;
Give me the strength never to disown the poor
or bend my knees before insolent might.
Give me the strength to raise my mind high
above daily trifles.
And give me the strength to surrender my
strength to Thy will with love.

Rabindranath Tagore (1861–1941)

O Lord, give us more charity, more self-denial, more likeness to You. Teach us to sacrifice our comforts to others, and our likings for the sake of doing good. Make us kindly in thought, gentle in word, generous in deed. Teach us that it is better to give than to receive, better to forget ourselves than to put ourselves forward, better to minister than to be ministered unto. And to You, God of love, be all glory and praise, now and forever. Amen.

Henry Alford (1810–1871)

Lord, baptize our hearts into a sense of the needs and conditions of all.

George Fox (1624–1691)

PRAYERS FOR TIMES OF ADVERSITY/SUFFERING

Give me my scallop shell of quiet,
My staff of faith to walk upon,
My scrip of joy, immortal diet,
My bottle of salvation,
My gown of glory, hope's true gage,
And thus I'll take my pilgrimage.

Sir Walter Raleigh (1552–1618),
just before his execution

THE BLESSING OF UNANSWERED PRAYERS

I asked for strength that I might achieve;
I was made weak that I might
learn humbly to obey.

I asked for health that I might do greater things;
I was given infirmity that I might do better things.
I asked for riches that I might be happy;
I was given poverty that I might be wise.
I asked for power that I might have the praise
of men;
I was given weakness that I might feel the need
of God.
I asked for all things that I might enjoy life;
I was given life that I might enjoy all things.
I got nothing that I had asked for,
but everything that I had hoped for.
Almost despite myself my unspoken prayers
were answered;
I am, among all men, most richly blessed.

Unknown Confederate Soldier

Grant that for Your sake I may come to love
and desire any hardship that puts me to the
test, for salvation is brought to my soul when I
undergo suffering and trouble for You.

Thomas à Kempis (1380–1471)

THE ALPHABET PRAYER

Although things are not perfect,
Because of trial or pain,
Continue in thanksgiving
Do not begin to blame;
Even when the times are hard,
Fierce winds are bound to blow,

God is forever able;
Hold on to what you know.
Imagine life without His love
Joy would cease to be,
Keep thanking Him for all the things
Love imparts to thee.
Move out of "Camp Complaining,"
No weapon that is known
On earth can yield the power
Praise can do alone.
Quit looking at the future,
Redeem the time at hand;
Start every day with worship,
To "thank" is a command.
Until we see Him coming
Victorious in the sky,
We'll run the race with gratitude
Xalting God most high.
Yes, there'll be good times
and yes, some will be bad,
but. . .Zion waits in glory. . .
Where none are ever sad!

Author Unknown

Help us to bear difficulty, pain,
disappointment, and sorrows, knowing that in
Your perfect working and design, You can use
such bitter experiences to shape our character
and make us more like our Lord.

Ignatius of Antioch (c. 30–107),
before his martyrdom

Lord God Almighty, the Father of Your well-beloved and blessed Son, Jesus Christ, by whom we have received knowledge of You, the God of angels and powers, and of every creature, and especially the whole race of just men who live in Your presence: I give thee hearty thanks that You have thought me worthy of this day and hours, to be numbered among Your martyrs, and to share in the cup of Christ, for resurrection to eternal life, for soul and body, in the incorruptibility of the Holy Spirit. Among them may I be accepted before You today, as a rich and acceptable sacrifice, just as You, the faithful and true God, have both ordained and prepared this day and also have now fulfilled it. For this reason, and for everything else, I praise You, bless You, and glorify You by the eternal and heavenly high priest, Jesus Christ, Your beloved Son, through whom be glory to You, with Him and the Holy Spirit, now and for the ages to come. Amen.

Polycarp (69–155),
as he awaited execution at the stake

Comfort, merciful Father, by Your word and the Holy Spirit, all who are afflicted or distressed, and so turn their hearts to You, that they may serve You in truth and bring forth fruit for Your glory.

Philip Melanchthon (1467–1560)

PRAYERS OF REPENTANCE/CONFESSION

O Lord, give us all, we beseech Thee, grace
and strength to overcome every sin; sins of
besetment, deliberation, surprise, negligence,
omission; sins against Thee, ourself, our
neighbor; sins great, small, remembered,
forgotten. Amen.

Christina Rossetti (1830–1895)

Almighty God, Father of mercies, be
pleased to work in me what Thou hast
commended should be in me. Give me, O
Lord, the grace of an earnest sorrow—turn
my sin into repentance, and let my repentance
proceed to pardon; and teach me so diligently
to watch over all my actions that I may never
transgress Thy holy laws willingly, but that
it may be the work of my life to obey Thee,
the joy of my soul to please Thee, and the
perfection of my desires to live with Thee in the
kingdom of Thy grace and glory. Amen.

Jeremy Taylor (1613–1667)

O Lord, my God, light of the blind and
strength of the weak; yea, also, light of those
that see, and strength of the strong; hearken
unto my soul, and hear it crying out of the
depths.

O Lord, help us to turn and seek Thee; for
Thou hast not forsaken Thy creatures as we

have forsaken Thee, our Creator. Let us turn and seek Thee, for we know Thou art here in our hearts, when we confess to Thee, when we cast ourselves upon Thee, and weep in Thy bosom, after all our rugged ways; and Thou dost gently wipe away our tears, and we weep the more for joy; because Thou, Lord, who madest us, dost remake and comfort us.

Hear, Lord, my prayer, and grant that I may most entirely love Thee, and do Thou rescue me, O Lord, from every temptation, even unto the end. Amen.

Augustine of Hippo (345–430)

O searcher of hearts, Thou knowest us better than we know ourselves, and seest the sins which our sinfulness hides from us. Yet even our own conscience beareth witness against us, that we often slumber on our appointed watch; that we walk not always lovingly with each other and humbly with Thee; and we withhold that entire sacrifice of ourselves to Thy perfect will, without which we are not crucified with Christ, or sharers in His redemption. Oh look upon our contrition and lift up our weakness, and let the dayspring yet arise within our hearts, and bring us healing, strength, and joy. Day by day may we grow in faith, in self-denial, in charity, in heavenly-mindedness. And then, mingle us at last with the mighty host of Thy redeemed forevermore. Amen.

James Martineau (1805–1900)

O merciful God, full of compassion, long-suffering and of great pity, make me earnestly repent and heartily to be sorry for all my misdoings; make the remembrance of them so burdensome and painful that I may flee to Thee with a troubled spirit and a contrite heart; and, O merciful Lord, visit, comfort, and relieve me; excite in me true repentance; give me in this world knowledge of Thy truth and confidence in Thy mercy, and, in the world to come, life everlasting. Strengthen me against sin, and enable so to perform every duty, that whilst I live I may serve Thee in that state to which Thou hast called me; and, at last, by a holy and happy death, be delivered from the struggles and sorrows of this life and obtain eternal happiness, for the sake of our Lord and Savior, Thy Son Jesus Christ. Amen.

Samuel Johnson (1709–1784)

O Thou gracious and gentle and condescending God, Thou God of peace, Father of mercy, God of all comfort; see, I lament before Thee the evil of my heart; I acknowledge that I am too much disposed to anger, jealousy, and revenge, to ambition and pride, which often give rise to discord and bitter feelings between me and others. Too often have I thus offended and grieved both Thee, O long-suffering Father, and my fellow men. Oh forgive me this sin, and suffer me to partake of the blessing which Thou hast promised to the peacemakers, who shall be called the children of God. Bestow on me, O Lord, a genial spirit and unwearied forbearance; a mild, loving, patient heart; kindly looks, pleasant, cordial speech and manners in the intercourse of daily life; that I may give offence to none, but as much as in me lies live in charity with all men. Amen.

Johann Arndt (1555–1621)

I offer up unto Thee my prayers and intercessions for those especially who have in any matter hurt, grieved, or found fault with me, or who have done me any damage or displeasure.

For all those also whom, at any time, I may have vexed, troubled, burdened, and scandalized, by words or deeds, knowingly or in ignorance; that Thou wouldst grant us all equally pardon for our sins, and for our offences against each other. Take away from our hearts, O Lord, all suspiciousness, indignation, wrath, and contention, and whatsoever may hurt charity and lessen brotherly love. Have mercy, O Lord, have mercy on those that crave Thy mercy; give grace unto them that stand in need thereof, and make us such as that we may be worthy to enjoy Thy grace and go forward to life eternal. Amen.

Thomas à Kempis (c. 1380–1471)

O Thou, who knowest our hearts, and who seest our temptations and struggles, have pity upon us, and deliver us from the sins which make war upon our souls. Thou art all-powerful and we are weak and erring. Our trust is in Thee, O Thou faithful and good God. Deliver us from the bondage of evil, and grant that we may thereafter be Thy devoted servants, serving Thee in the freedom of holy love, for Christ's sake. Amen.

Eugène Bersier (1830–1903)

O sweet Savior Christ, in Your undeserved love for us You were prepared to suffer the painful death of the cross: let me not be cold or even lukewarm in my love for You. Lord, help me to face the truth about myself. Help me to hear my words as others hear them, to see my face as others see me; let me be honest enough to recognize my impatience and conceit; let me recognize my anger and selfishness; give me sufficient humility to accept my own weaknesses for what they are. Give me the grace—at least in Your presence—to say, "I was wrong—forgive me." God, the Father of our Lord Jesus Christ, increase in us faith and truth and gentleness and grant us part and lot among the saints.

Polycarp (69–155)

DEAR LORD AND FATHER OF MANKIND (ABRIDGED)

Dear Lord and Father of mankind,
Forgive our foolish ways!
Reclothe us in our rightful mind,
In purer lives Thy service find,
In deeper reverence, praise.

Drop Thy still dews of quietness,
Till all our strivings cease;
Take from our souls the strain and stress,
And let our ordered lives confess
The beauty of Thy peace.

Breathe through the heat of our desire
Thy coolness and Thy balm;
Let sense be dumb, let flesh retire;
Speak through the earthquake, wind, and
    fire,
O still, small voice of calm!
        John Greenleaf Whittier (1807–1892)

Most merciful Father, we come before Your throne in the name of Jesus Christ, that for His sake alone You will have compassion on us, and not let our sins be a cloud between You and us.
        John Colet (1467(?)–1519)

Forgive them all, O Lord; our sins of omission and our sins of commission; the sins of our youth and the sins of our riper years; the sins of our souls and the sins of our bodies; our secret and our more open sins; our sins of ignorance and surprise, and our more deliberate and presumptuous sin; the sins we have done to please ourselves, and the sins we have done to please others; the sins we know and remember and the sins we have forgotten; the sins we have striven to hide from others and the sins by which we have made others offend. Forgive them, O Lord, forgive them all for His sake, who died for our sins and rose for our justification and now stands at Thy right hand to make intercession for us, Jesus Christ our Lord.

John Wesley (1662–1735)

Almighty, forgive my doubt, my anger, my pride. By Your mercy abase me, in Your strictness raise me up.

Dag Hammarskjöld (1905–1961)

7

Not Your "Everyday" Prayers
PRAYERS FOR HOLIDAYS/SPECIAL OCCASIONS

CHRISTMAS PRAYERS

Loving Father, help us remember the birth of Jesus, that we may share in the song of the angels, the gladness of the shepherds, and worship of the wise men.

Close the door of hate and open the door of love all over the world. Let kindness come with every gift and good desires with every greeting. Deliver us from evil by the blessing which Christ brings, and teach us to be merry with clear hearts.

May the Christmas morning make us happy to be Thy children, and Christmas evening bring us to our beds with grateful thoughts, forgiving and forgiven, for Jesus' sake. Amen.

Robert Louis Stevenson (1850–1894)

We yearn, our Father, for the simple beauty of Christmas—for all the old familiar melodies and words that remind us of that great miracle when He who had made all things was one night to come as a babe, to lie in the crook of a woman's arm.

Before such mystery we kneel, as we follow

the shepherds and wise men to bring Thee
the gift of our love—a love we confess has not
always been as warm or sincere or real as it
should have been. But now, on this Christmas
Day, that love would find its Beloved, and from
Thee receive the grace to make it pure again,
warm and real.

We bring Thee our gratitude for every
token of Thy love, for all the ways Thou hast
heaped blessings upon us during the years that
have gone.

And we do pray, Lord Jesus, that as we
celebrate Thy birthday, we may do it in a
manner well pleasing to Thee. May all we
do and say, every tribute of our hearts, bring
honor to Thy name, that we, Thy people, may
remember Thy birth and feel Thy presence
among us even yet.

May the loving-kindness of Christmas not
only creep into our hearts, but there abide, so
that not even the return to earthly cares and
responsibilities, not all the festivities of our own
devising may cause it to creep away weeping.
May the joy and spirit of Christmas stay with
us now and forever.

In the name of Jesus, who came to save His
people from their sins, even in that lovely name
we pray. Amen.

Peter Marshall (1902–1942)

Moonless darkness stands between.
Past, the past, no more be seen!
But the Bethlehem star may lead me
To the sight of Him who freed me
From the self that I have been.
Make me pure, Lord: Thou art holy;
Make me meek, Lord: Thou wert lowly;
Now beginning, and alway:
Now begin, on Christmas Day.

Gerard Manley Hopkins (1844–1889)

Good Jesus, born at this time, a little child
of love for us: be born in me so that I may be a
little child in love with You.

Edward Bouverie Pusey (1800–1882)

As on this day we keep the special memory
of our Redeemer's entry into the city, so grand,
Lord, that now and ever he may triumph in our
hearts. Let the king of grace and glory enter in,
and let us lay ourselves and all we are in the full
joyful homage before him.

H. C. G. Moule (1841–1920)

Ah, dearest Jesus, holy child,
Make thee a bed, soft, undefiled,
Within my heart, that it may be
A quiet chamber kept for Thee.

My heart for very joy doth leap,
My lips no more can silence keep,
I, too, must sing, with joyful tongue,
That sweetest ancient song,

Glory to God in highest heaven,
Who unto man His Son hath given
While angels sing with pious mirth.
A glad new year to all the earth!
Martin Luther (1483–1546)

How silently, how silently,
the wondrous Gift is giv'n;
So God imparts to human hearts
the blessings of His heav'n.
No ear may hear His coming,
but in this world of sin,
Where meek souls will receive Him still, the
dear Christ enters in.

O holy child of Bethlehem,
descend to us, we pray;
Cast out our sin, and enter in,
be born in us today.
We hear the Christmas angels
the great glad tidings tell;
O come to us, abide with us,
our Lord Emmanuel!
Philips Brooks (1835–1893),
from "O Little Town of Bethlehem"

Let Your goodness, Lord, appear to us, that we made in Your image, conform ourselves to it.

In our own strength we cannot imitate Your majesty, power, and wonder; nor is it fitting for us to try. But Your mercy reaches from the heavens through the clouds to the earth below. You have come to us as a small child, but you have brought us the greatest of all gifts, the gift of eternal love; caress us with Your tiny hands, embrace us with Your tiny arms and pierce our hearts with Your soft, sweet cries.

Bernard of Clairvaux (1090–1153)

Loving God, we give thanks for the birth of Your Son Jesus Christ, both in human form in Bethlehem and in spiritual form in our hearts. May He reign as king within every human heart, so that every town and village can live according to His joyful law of love.

Thomas Münzer (1490–1525)

GOOD FRIDAY

Good Friday in My Heart

Good Friday in my heart! Fear and affright!
My thoughts are the disciples when they fled,
My words the words that priest and soldier said,
My deed the spear to desecrate the dead.
And day, Thy death therein, is changed to night.

Then Easter in my heart sends up the sun.
My thoughts are Mary, when she turned to see.
My words are Peter, answering, 'Lov'st thou Me?'
My deeds are all Thine own drawn close to Thee,
And night and day, since Thou dost rise, are one.

Mary Elizabeth Coleridge (1861–1907)

Jesus, You let your side be opened by the
spear so that there could come forth blood
and water; wound my heart with the spear of
charity so that I may be made worthy of Your
sacraments which flow from Your most holy
side.

Ludolf of Saxony (c. 1300–c. 1378)

Almighty and eternal God, merciful Father,
who has given to the human race Your beloved
Son as an example of humility, obedience,
and patience, to precede us on the way of life,
bearing the cross: graciously grant that we be
inflamed by His infinite love so that way may
take up the sweet yoke of His gospel, following
Him as His true disciples, so that we shall one
day gloriously rise with Him and joyfully hear
the final sentence: "Come, you blessed of My
Father, and possess the kingdom which was
prepared for you from the beginning," where
You reign with the Son and the Holy Ghost,
and where we hope to reign with You, world
without end.

Francis of Assisi (1181–1226)

Grant, Lord, that in Your wounds I may find my safety, in Your stripes my cure, in Your pain my peace, in Your cross my victory, in Your resurrection my triumph.

Jeremy Taylor (1613–1667)

Easter (Resurrection Day)

It is only right, with all the powers of our heart and mind, to praise You, Father, and Your only begotten Son, our Lord Jesus Christ: dear Father, by Your wondrous condescension of loving-kindness toward us, Your servants, You gave up Your Son.

Dear Jesus, You paid the debt of Adam for us to the eternal Father by Your blood poured forth in loving-kindness. You cleared away the darkness of sin by Your magnificent and radiant resurrection. You broke the bonds of death and rose from the grave as a conqueror.

You reconciled heaven and earth. Our life had no hope of eternal happiness before You redeemed us. Your resurrection has washed away our sins, restored our innocence, and brought us joy.

How inestimable is the tenderness of Your love!

Gregory the Great (540–604)

O God, who for our redemption gave Your only begotten Son to the death of the cross, and by His glorious resurrection delivered us from the power of our enemy: grant us so to die daily to sin, that we may evermore live with Him in the joy of His resurrection.

Anglican Easter Prayer

I see flames of orange, yellow, and red shooting upward to the sky, piercing the whole clouds. I see the clouds themselves chasing the flames upward, and I feel the air itself reaching for the heavens.

Down below I see great, gray rocks beating against the earth, as if they were pushing their way down to hell.

At Your resurrection, that which is light and good rises up with You, and that which is heavy and evil is pushed downward.

At Your resurrection, goodness breaks from evil, life breaks free from death.

The Victorines

Almighty God, who through the death of Your Son has destroyed sin and death and by His resurrection has restored the innocence and everlasting life so we could be saved from the power of the devil, and so our mortal bodies raised up from the dead: grant that we may confidently and wholeheartedly believe this message and that, finally, we may share with Your saints in the joyful resurrection of those who have been justified through You.

Martin Luther (1483–1546)

BIRTHDAYS

Almighty and everlasting God, the maker of all creation: mercifully hear our prayer and grant many and happy years to Your servant whose birthday it is, that he may spend all his life so as to please You, through Jesus Christ our Lord.

The Gelasian Sacramentary (8th Century)

Eternal Father, the giver of life, who on this day caused Your servant to be born into this world: we thank You, Lord, for all Your mercies granted to him from that time until now and humbly ask You to continue Your gracious favor and protection until his life's end. Help him in every time of trial, shield him in danger, relieve and comfort him in trouble, assist him against temptation, defend him from the assaults of the enemy, so that his days here may pass in peace so that when he dies, he may attain unto the everlasting rest that remains for Your people.

William Edward Scudamore (1813–1881)

BAPTISM

Look down from heaven, Lord, upon Your flock and Your lambs. Bless their bodies and their souls, and grant that those who have received the sign of the cross on their foreheads at baptism may be shown to belong to You on the day of judgment, through Jesus Christ our Lord.

Egbert of York (d. 766)

Make Yourself manifest, Lord, in this water, and grant to him who is baptized in it so to be transformed that he may put off the old man, which is corrupted by deceitful lusts, and may put on the new man, which is formed fresh according to the image of the Creator. Grafted through baptism into the likeness of Your death, may he become a partaker also in Your resurrection. May he guard the gift of Your Holy Spirit, may he increase in the measure of grace, which has been entrusted to him, and may he receive the prize which is God's calling to life above, being numbered among the firstborn whose names are written in heaven.

Eastern Orthodox Baptismal

Almighty and eternal God, most merciful Father, as the just live by faith and as it is impossible for anyone to please You without faith, we pray that You will grant to this child the gift of faith, in which You will seal and assure his heart in the Holy Spirit, according to the promise of Your Son; that the inner regeneration of the Spirit may be truly represented by the outward baptism, and that the child may be buried with Christ into death and be raised up from death by Christ, to the praise of Your glory and the building up of his neighbor.

Miles Coverdale (1488–1568)

Lord of the flood, wash us with Your Spirit that we may be Your ark of life, Your peace in the sea of violence. Water is life; water cleans; water kills. Frightened, we are tempted to make a permanent home on the ark. But You force us to seek dry ground. We can do so only because You have taught us to cling to our baptisms, when we are drowned and reborn by the water and fire of Your Spirit. So reborn, make us unafraid. Amen.

Stanley Hauerwas (b. 1940)

WEDDINGS/MARRIAGE

Wedding Blessing

God, the best maker of all marriages,
combine your hearts in one,
your realms in one.

William Shakespeare (1564–1616)

Blessed be the light that has guided your souls to the threshold of this new day.

Blessed be the journey you walk as one sharing your love with the world.

Blessed be the stillness that refreshes your souls and awakens God's dream in your hearts.

The shield of the God of life be yours.

The compassion of the loving Christ be
yours.

The wisdom of the living Spirit be yours.
Now and evermore.

Celtic Christian Wedding Blessing

Most gracious God, we give You thanks
for Your tender love in sending Jesus Christ
to come among us, to be born of a human
mother, and to make the way of the cross to
be the way of life. We thank You, also, for
consecrating the union of man and woman in
His name.

By the power of Your Holy Spirit, pour
out the abundance of Your blessing upon this
man and this woman. Defend them from every
enemy. Lead them into all peace. Let their
love for each other be a seal upon their hearts,
a mantle about their shoulders, and a crown
upon their foreheads. Bless them in their work
and in their companionship; in their sleeping
and in their waking; in their joys and in their
sorrows; in their life and in their death.

Finally, in Your mercy, bring them to that
table where Your saints feast forever in Your
heavenly home; through Jesus Christ our Lord,
who with You and the Holy Spirit lives and
reigns, one God, forever and ever. Amen.

Book of Common Prayer

Lord, help us to remember when we first
met and the strong love that grew between us.
   To work that love into practical things so
nothing can divide us. We ask for words both
kind and loving and for hearts always ready to
ask forgiveness as well as to forgive. Dear Lord,
we put our marriage into Your hands. Amen.

                                    Author Unknown

WEDDING PRAYER

Lord, behold our family here assembled.
We thank You for this place in which we dwell,
            for the love that unites us,
      for the peace accorded us this day,
for the hope with which we expect the morrow,
        for the health, the work, the food,
     and the bright skies that make our lives
                     delightful;
    for our friends in all parts of the earth.
                      Amen.
            Robert Louis Stevenson (1850–1894)

BEREAVEMENT/FUNERALS

Catholic Funeral Prayer

God our Father,
Your power brings us to birth,
Your providence guides our lives,
and by Your command we return to dust.
Lord, those who die still live in Your presence,

their lives change but do not end.
I pray in hope for my family,
relatives, and friends,
and for all the dead known to You alone.
In company with Christ,
Who died and now lives,
may they rejoice in Your kingdom,
where all our tears are wiped away.
Unite us together again in one family,
to sing Your praise forever and ever.
Amen.

Ah, poor lonely widow and miserable
woman that I am, may He who does not
forsake widows and orphans console me. O my
God, console me! O my Jesus, strengthen me in
my weakness!

Elizabeth of Hungary (1207–1231),
after the death of her husband

If Death My Friend and Me Divide

If death my friend and me divide,
Thou dost not, Lord, my sorrow chide,
Or frown my tears to see;
Restrained from passionate excess,
Thou bidst me mourn in calm distress
For them that rest in Thee.

I feel a strong immortal hope,
Which bears my mournful spirit up

Beneath its mountain load;
Redeemed from death, and grief, and pain,
I soon shall find my friend again

Within the arms of God.
Pass a few fleeting moments more
And death the blessing shall restore
Which death has snatched away;
For me Thou wilt the summons send,
And give me back my parted friend
In that eternal day.

Charles Wesley (1707–1788)

O God, to me who am left to mourn his
departure, grant that I may not sorrow as one
without hope for my beloved who sleeps in
You; but as always remembering his courage
and the love that united us on earth, I may
begin again with new courage to serve You
more fervently who are the only source of true
love and true fortitude that when I have passed
a few more days in this valley of tears and
this shadow of death, supported by Your rod
and staff, I may see him face to face, in those
pastures and beside those waters of comfort
where I believe he already walks with You.
O Shepherd of the sheep, have pity on this
darkened soul of mine.

Edward White Benson (1829–1896),
after the death of his young son

God of all consolation, in Your unending love and mercy for us, You turn the darkness of death into the dawn of new life.

Show compassion to Your people in their sorrow, be our refuge and our strength, to lift us from the darkness of this grief to the peace and light of Your presence.

Your Son, our Lord Jesus Christ, by dying for us, conquered death, and by rising again, restored to us eternal life: may we then go forward eagerly to meet our Redeemer and, after our life on earth, be reunited with all our brothers and sisters in that place where every tear is wiped away and all things are made new, through Jesus Christ our Savior.

The Roman Catholic *Family Prayer Book*

It Is Well with My Soul

When peace, like a river, attendeth my way,
When sorrows like sea billows roll;
Whatever my lot, Thou has taught me to say,
It is well, it is well, with my soul.

It is well, with my soul,
It is well, with my soul,
It is well, it is well, with my soul.

Though Satan should buffet,
though trials should come,
Let this blest assurance control,

That Christ has regarded my helpless estate,
And hath shed His own blood for my soul.

It is well, with my soul,
It is well, with my soul,
It is well, it is well, with my soul.

My sin, oh, the bliss of this glorious thought!
My sin, not in part but the whole,
Is nailed to the cross, and I bear it no more,
Praise the Lord, praise the Lord, O my soul!

It is well, with my soul,
It is well, with my soul,
It is well, it is well, with my soul.

And Lord, haste the day when
my faith shall be sight,
The clouds be rolled back as a scroll;
The trump shall resound, and the Lord shall
descend,
Even so, it is well with my soul.

It is well, with my soul,
It is well, with my soul,
It is well, it is well, with my soul.
Horatio G. Spafford (1828–1888),
after the tragic death of his four daughters